Corporate Strategies for Social Performance

CORPORATE STRATEGIES
FOR
SOCIAL PERFORMANCE

Melvin Anshen

Studies of the Modern Corporation
Graduate School of Business
Columbia University

MACMILLAN PUBLISHING CO., INC.
NEW YORK

Collier Macmillan Publishers
LONDON

Macmillan Publishing Co., Inc.
866 Third Avenue, New York, N.Y. 10022

Collier Macmillan Canada, Ltd.

Library of Congress Catalog Card Number: 79–7888

Printed in the United States of America

printing number

3 4 5 6 7 8 9 10

Library of Congress Cataloging in Publication Data

Anshen, Melvin.
    Corporate strategies for social performance.

    (Studies of the modern corporation)
    Includes index.
    1. Industry--Social aspects. I. Title. II. Series.
HD60.A568 1980   658.4'08   79-7888
ISBN 0-02-900730-5

THE PROGRAM FOR STUDIES
OF
THE MODERN CORPORATION

Graduate School of Business, Columbia University

The Program for Studies of the Modern Corporation is devoted to the advancement and dissemination of knowledge about the corporation. Its publications are designed to stimulate inquiry, research, criticism, and reflection. They fall into three categories: works by outstanding businessmen, scholars, and professional men from a variety of backgrounds and academic disciplines; annotated and edited selections of business literature; and business classics that merit republication. The studies are supported by outside grants from private business, professional, and philanthropic institutions interested in the program's objectives.

RICHARD EELLS
Director

Contents

Contents

CONTENTS

Preface

THE reason for undertaking this book is that, although there has been a growing volume of writing and talking about corporate social responsibility, emanating from both supporters and critics of the concept, very little attention has been directed to the practical problems of managing corporate social performance.

These are not simple problems. They range from deciding what social performance policies and activities are desirable and feasible for a company to adopt all the way to deciding how to implement approved programs effectively and efficiently. The arena in which these problems are encountered extends from the board of directors and the chief executive officer at the top of the organization structure to the lowest level of supervision. And the problems involve sensitive and complex internal relationships among levels of management, and between managers and nonmanagement employees, and also relationships between a company and its various external publics: customers, interest groups, communities, national and local governmental organizations and officials, and the vaguely defined yet ultimately powerful "general public."

This book is therefore principally concerned with issues of what to do and how to do it. The chosen focus reflects the primary concern of Mr. Paul Garrett, whose perceptive understanding of critical problems at the business-society interface and of the need for clarifying the role of corporate leadership in managing this sensitive relationship was the motivation for his generous gift to Columbia University in 1971, which endowed a professorship in Public Policy and Business Responsibility. From his experiences during twenty-five years as Vice President–Public Relations of the General Motors Corporation, Mr. Garrett developed the conclusion that business organizations, which are franchised by their host society, must be responsive to society's expectations for their behavior. But beyond that degree of minimum responsiveness needed to comply with mandated behavior, he envisioned a broader business responsibility to anticipate emerging social needs and to act constructively to help society accomplish its goals. And he believed that business leaders have an obligation to society and to their organizations to be creative in formulating these actions and vigorous in implementing them.

In working through the ideas incorporated in this book, I have been continually stimulated, challenged, and refreshed by discussions with Dr. Courtney C. Brown, Dean Emeritus of Columbia's Graduate School of Business and the first Garrett Professor of Public Policy and Business Responsibility. His lively interest in corporate social performance and his conviction that social performance is inextricably linked with economic performance have been valuable resources at every stage of my work on the book.

MELVIN ANSHEN
Paul Garrett, Professor of Public Policy
    and Business Responsibility
Columbia University
January 1980

1

A New Social Contract for Business

THE following statement appeared in a perceptive and provocative pamphlet published in 1973: ". . . if business corporations are to adjust to continually changing demands for social as well as economic performance, they must do something more fundamental than respond to the proposals of others. Business must restructure its objectives so that social goals are put on a par with economic goals."[1]

The force of the statement is dramatically emphasized by its source. The Council on Trends and Perspective of the Chamber of Commerce of the United States is not a group of social revolutionaries or utopian dreamers. What the Council was concerned about was not simply the appearance and growth of new concepts about the proper role and behavior of business organizations in our society, concepts that were finding expression along the range from expectations to demands to legislation and regulation prohibiting or mandating specific business conduct. It was also interested in exploring ways and means by which corporations and their managers could participate constructively in defining feasible business roles and behavior patterns in our evolving society, and in designing effective and efficient machinery for their implementation.

A similar idea was articulated by David Rockefeller in a 1971 address to the Advertising Council in which he predicted a future requirement for corporations to publish certified audits of their social performance in annual reports to stockholders: "It is vital that social accountability become an integral part of corporate conduct, rather than a philanthropic add-on. Only in that way will the economic development of the private sector move forward within an acceptable framework of public purpose. Only in that way will corporations assure the healthy social climate vital to their own future economic prosperity."[2] A comparable position was outlined in two publications of the Committee for Economic Development,[3] and by a growing number of business leaders, educators, politicians, and other observers of social developments and trends.

The implications of the Chamber of Commerce statement are complex and critically important. They are, in the literal meaning of the word, revolutionary. Restructuring business objectives to put social goals on a par with economic goals will require radical transformation of the theory and practice of the private enterprise system. It will require massive changes in every phase of business management from long-range planning to daily operations. It will reorganize priorities in the allocation and use of all types of resources. It will call for redesign of systems for measuring and controlling activities, for analyzing costs and benefits, and for public reporting of business performance. It will influence decisions that affect every aspect of an enterprise: all functions, including research, production, marketing, finance, and personnel; all levels of management from the board of directors through senior officers down to first-line supervisors; relations with all publics—employees, customers, suppliers, shareowners, financing institutions, plant communities, and governmental institutions, and their staffs from national to local levels. Above all, it will require corporate managers to evaluate and choose among optional strategies with the knowledge that the selected option may well determine the continuing health of both the business sector and the total society in which it has been such an important and dynamic element.

Levels of Analysis: Conceptual to Operational

The critical issues present themselves on three interrelated levels of analysis. The first level is that of philosophy and concept. Should corporate managers be concerned at all with defining a social role for business institutions? Is it appropriate and advantageous for them to think of themselves as responsible for the social as well as the economic results of their administration of resources? Is such a responsibility, translated into the reality of performance, compatible with a profit-oriented enterprise system? In the broadest terms, will the benefits justify the costs, assuming the possibility of even crude assessment of benefits and costs? Is private gain compatible with social gain when social gain is calculated in terms broader than the GNP arithmetic? And possibly the most fundamental of all questions: do managers have a meaningful choice, or are they, for better or worse, moving in the current of a social change so powerful as to deny control, influence, or even effective resistance?

The second level of analysis is that of corporate planning. During the past twenty years the art and technology of planning have developed rapidly in scope, sophistication, and embodiment in administrative systems. With only marginal exceptions, however, planning has been oriented toward economic performance in terms of the investment of economic resources to accomplish economic goals. To place social goals on a par with economic goals will require, first, the definition of social goals for the individual business, and second, the development of a calculus for monitoring and evaluating the interactions between economic and social performance. These are extraordinarily difficult requirements. They call for innovation in the structure, the arithmetic, and the organizational politics of planning. They introduce a new dimension in management thinking about a corporation's future—a dimension that is relatively unfamiliar to most managers, one that cannot fail to challenge the values and the systems they accept and with which they feel comfortable.

The third level of analysis is that of management process and practice. From top to bottom of the organization there will be inescapable changes in how the work gets done. The board of directors is a target for pressures urging redesign of its membership and its control over the selection of members, its responsibilities (perhaps, more accurately, its performance of statutory and operational responsibilities that have generally been underfulfilled), its agenda, its access to operating information, its participation in the strategic planning process, its implementation of the audit function, and its sensitivity to

4

the implications of developments in the external environment.

Senior line management must broaden its decision-making horizons, open channels for inbound communications—both descriptive and interpretive—about social attitudes and forces relevant for current and future business behavior, and evaluate and provide policy and procedural guidance for all phases of internal operations, including environmental impact, safety and hygiene of working conditions, product safety and performance, personnel administration, and adherence to approved standards of legal and ethical conduct. In addition, senior management must develop or acquire competence in handling relations with governmental organizations and their staffs, an area in which most executives have been distinguished for performance ranging from mediocre to inept. Middle managers and even first-level supervisors must be educated and motivated to accept and implement policies, programs, and practices that stretch the boundaries of their traditional responsibilities and skills.

All of this raises a formidable challenge to management imagination and talent. Yet it is precisely what is required if social goals are to be put on a par with economic goals. Whether managers view it as a threat to be avoided or defeated, or as an opportunity to be examined and exploited, probably will be determined by their judgments about the character and causes of the public's disenchantment with and criticism of corporate behavior and the general erosion of public confidence in business institutions and their leaders. Is this a temporary phenomenon, or does it reflect a transformation of broadly based public attitudes that is likely to endure? The answer to this question will be a key determinant of a rational business strategy.

The Idea of a Contract between Society and Business

American business institutions function within a social system. The system confers legitimacy on business institutions, defines the bounds and rules of their performance, and in a variety of ways evaluates the aggregate cost-benefit trade-off that is the result of business activity. The conclusion is inescapable that the corporation receives its permission to operate from the society and ultimately is accountable to the society for what it does and how it does it.

In our pluralistic democracy the social will that ultimately determines what business organizations do and how they do it is expressed in a variety of ways: by general and specific legislation, by regulation pursuant to legislative mandate, by judicial review and interpretation of legislation and regulation, and by informal expressions of needs, expectations, and demands. "Social will" must be understood, of course, as shorthand for whatever consensus emerges from the interplay of multiple disparate interests and pressures. The whole process is partly legalistic, often informal, sometimes chaotic, on occasion irrational and self-damaging, at times inconsistent or capricious. It is easy to be critical of the democratic process, as Winston Churchill observed, until one considers the alternatives.

The process is dynamic. The social will changes through time, responding to perceived evolving needs and desires. Business legitimacy once conferred may be revoked. The bounds and rules of business operations may be revised. The criteria that govern the popular assessment of the trade-offs between the costs and benefits of business activities may be modified. Even concepts that define costs and benefits are not stable.

In this fluid situation, there is at any given time a

prevailing set of expectations for business behavior that can be usefully viewed as a "contract" between society and business. If the word suggests unduly rigid or legalistic overtones to a corporate manager, he may prefer to think of it as a set of understandings. However tightly or loosely described, the ultimate sanctions of social power are always present and cannot be avoided. These are the rules of the game, and the players must recognize and comply with them. The players are not prohibited from trying to change the rules, by working within the democratic process, but they are governed by the prevailing rules until the rules are revised through any of several operative mechanisms ranging from formal legislation to informal acceptance of innovative practice.

The Old Contract

Such a contract between business institutions and the enveloping society existed almost unchanged from the start of the American Republic until recently. Under the terms of this historic contract, society stipulated that business should operate freely in response to the motivation of profit maximization, subject only to marginal constraints. Economic growth, feeding a rising standard of living, was widely accepted as the source of all progress—social as well as economic. The only significant restriction laid upon business was that it must be competitive, and this rule was not formalized until the latter part of the nineteenth century.

Under the contract, through most of the period, society laid no compulsion upon private business to recognize and bear what are now viewed as the external costs of its operations: unemployment, unpensioned retirement, environmental contamination, hazardous working conditions, inequitable personnel practices, deception or injury of consumers. These were not recognized as business costs. In the broadest terms, the contract stipulated that business organizations collectively and individually bore no responsibility for the general social welfare or for the specific conditions of daily life in the nation as a whole and in local communities.

For almost two centuries the United States experienced an economic expansion possibly unparalleled in the world's history. The absence of restrictions on business activity, the availability of a seemingly limitless supply of relatively cheap resources, and access to a large and expanding national market combined to create extraordinarily favorable conditions for economic growth. With the exception of a handful of critics, no one seriously questioned the social benefits of this economic growth or even suggested that important social costs were not recognized and accounted for.

The New Contract

Probably the most significant element in the social contract whose provisions have begun to be visible in recent years is a shift in the perceived relationship between economic and social benefits—in the popular phrase, between "the quantity of life and the quality of life." We are becoming sensitive as a society to the unpleasant and sometimes wounding by-products of unrestricted economic growth. We are beginning to be concerned about economic and social burdens not recorded in the accounting records of business organizations and not reflected in their costs and prices. Increasingly, this concern is feeding a popular demand that corporations internalize their social costs, that they make positive contributions to minimizing or removing environmental contamination and dangerous and unhealthy working conditions, that they assure to their customers the quality and safety of their products, and that they act affirmatively to provide equal access to jobs and careers to members of all groups in our society.

The social attitudes reflected in the emerging contract in effect stipulate that business can no longer justify its existence by reference to either the natural or legal rights of private property, or to its economic performance in creating a rising standard of living as measured by gross national product (GNP). The legitimacy of business is now challenged on the grounds that some of its activities are making our society ugly, dirty, polluted, and dangerous, and that business is acting as a powerful institution for perpetuating economic and social inequities. Rather than being seen as Adam Smith's "invisible hand" maximizing public benefits, profit-oriented private decisions are now often viewed as antisocial in character. It is irrelevant to observe that some of these popular judgments are inaccurate, unbalanced, or biased. The important fact is that these judgments exist and are contributing to the formulation of new standards for corporate behavior. The judgments are expressed by activist leaders and groups, by general articulation of widespread public opinion, and, if business response is found deficient, by specific acts of legislation and regulation.

This set of evolving attitudes is the underlying cause of the loss of respect for and growth of hostility to business institutions and their managers. Corporations used to be perceived as economic institutions. Now they are also viewed as social, cultural, and political institutions. This emerging view is the source of the growing demand for revised standards for business behavior. In effect, perceptions of a malperforming business system, as judged by a newly emerging set of values, are encouraging a new definition of the responsibilities of the enterprise system and new criteria for determining acceptable performance.

It is precisely because these issues have not been handled by traditional economic theory and analysis that someone like Professor Milton Friedman, who comes at social performance from the intellectual position of economics, can argue that business should not and must not deviate from its profit orientation and that it should be concerned only with its economic performance. What the emerging social contract is saying is that profit seeking must be carried on within a broader context than the traditional economic calculus, that the corporation is a social organization as well as an economic organization and its performance will be appraised in social as well as economic terms.

If one believes that many of today's social pressures identify a society in transition to a new value system, one that embraces social as well as economic performance, an effective business strategy requires a broader horizon than the traditional determinants of corporate policy and practice. One thing we ought to know for sure: what the majority of members of a democratic society want, they will ultimately get—even if at a price some might not have been willing to pay had they been aware of its magnitude.

The Significance of New Social Expectations for Business Performance

The emerging revised expectations for business performance cannot rationally be assessed as either trivial or alien to the normal business decision-making process.

The fact that they broaden the context of management decisions to embrace social as well as economic costs and benefits complicates the task but does not change its inherent character. As Neil H. Jacoby observed, social (including political) forces are as potent determinants of corporate strategy as are traditional market forces.[4] They help to explain actual business behavior, provide a valid basis for predicting business behavior, and delineate the norms for enlightened profit-oriented business decisions. Dr. Jacoby concluded that social forces are susceptible to the same type of cost-benefit analysis that is regularly applied to economic forces and that long-run profit maximization can be accomplished only through a comprehensive approach that merges social and economic considerations.

Those who share this view may well conclude that objections raised by critics of the concept of corporate social performance are empty arguments. It is no longer a question of whether business should accept any responsibilities to society other than its classic responsibility of contributing to the general welfare by pursuing maximum profits within the law. Rather, the critical issues are identifying (1) what responses to social needs can feasibly be undertaken by a single company under the constraints of its unique competitive position and unique resources, (2) what responses are feasible only through some type of cooperative effort among firms in a single industry or geographic location, and (3) what responses require some type of governmental intervention to which business may be able to contribute valuable guidance.

This point of view is beginning to make its way through the very top echelon of corporate management. Not long after the publications on this subject sponsored by the Committee for Economic Development and the Chamber

11

of Commerce of the United States, the Urban Affairs Committee of the National Association of Manufacturers published a report, *Corporations and Social Responsibility,* in which Augustine R. Marusi, board chairman of Borden Inc., said: "I feel that as businessmen we must do more to anticipate the needs of our society. I don't think we fully discharge our social responsibility by facing up to and attempting to solve problems as they arise. We have an obligation to work with government—and all other groups in our society—to see that they never come up in the first place." Mr. Marusi went on to describe three stages in attaining full corporate social performance. The first stage is to assure that activities responsive to social needs are made a permanent and integral part of corporate operations. The second stage is to get all levels of management fully involved so that policies and programs adopted at the top of the organization are effectively and efficiently implemented. The third stage will be reached when business leaders stop thinking about social responsibility and start thinking about social opportunity.

This issue is on the desk of every chief executive officer. He is inescapably charged with the duty of scanning the total external environment in which the business operates, evaluating that environment to identify the opportunities and threats it presents for his business, and determining the policies and strategies that will chart and run a successful course for the business through the environment. With an environment broadened from traditional economic considerations to include issues of social cost and social performance, the job of the chief executive officer obviously becomes more complex. It requires knowledge and skills beyond those previously essential for successful performance of his leadership responsibility.

Fundamental Questions in Determining Corporate Responses to Social Needs

In determining how to respond to perceived public expectations and demands for corporate social performance, both general for all business and specific to his company, the chief executive officer faces two familiar fundamental questions. These are the same two questions he has regularly faced in fulfilling his traditional responsibility for corporate economic performance. The first question is, What is it desirable and feasible for this company to do? More fully, what policies and programs should we adopt that will respond positively and constructively to social requirements, that our resources will permit us to undertake, and that will strengthen—or at least will not weaken—our economic position and prospects? The second question is: How can we organize available resources so that whatever we decide to do in this area will be accomplished effectively and efficiently? Although the questions are familiar, the answers are not. Some of the applicable analytical tools and methods can be borrowed from standard management analysis. There is also a requirement, however, for new analytical tools, new knowledge, and new skills.

It should be recognized at the outset that it is not desirable or even possible for a single corporation to respond to all the demands and expectations generated by outside interests, groups, and individuals along the full range of social performance. The individual firm can take constructive action on its own for only selected items on a list that includes environmental hygiene, product performance and safety, hiring and career equity, safety and hygiene of the work place and process, contributions to the amelioration of the massive problems and discontents of urban communities, and whatever else might be added.

13

This limitation should not be allowed to be the end of the matter, however. If the chief executive officer believes the proposition advanced earlier in this chapter that what a popular majority, or even an organized and politically aggressive minority, intensively desires and persists in trying to get it will ultimately attain, albeit often in socially undesirable ways and with unnecessary or even intolerable costs, then he cannot fail to be concerned about what may happen to a business system that is widely viewed as unresponsive to the social will. Accepting this proposition, the perceptive chief executive officer should then be prepared to consider how to organize constructive business responses that exceed the feasibility limits of action by his organization alone.

Strategic Options in Choosing Responses to Social Needs

In evaluating desirable and feasible responses to social expectations and demands, the corporate manager may usefully distinguish among three optional strategies. The first is unilateral action by his company. The second is coordinated or cooperative action by all or the leading companies in a single industry or single geographic location. The third strategy encompasses initiatives aimed at securing or influencing appropriate legislative or administrative action by some level of government. Each of these three strategies can be specifically related to a set of conditions that define the limits of feasibility for corporate action. Determining these limits is essential for the executive who is genuinely concerned about moving from concept to practice in social performance.

The circumstances that create a favorable situation for unilateral action by a single company have two principal

14

characteristics. The first is that they permit the design and execution of a program that will produce significant positive results—results that can be described, measured at least roughly, and reported, if desired, to various publics. The second characteristic is that the activity will not incur costs that would adversely affect the company's competitive position or financial performance. In the best of all possible worlds, the activity should also present an interesting probability of generating a profitable long-run return on the resources committed to its accomplishment.

For obvious reasons, it is critically important to be thoroughly realistic in appraising the competitive cost implications of any proposed socially responsive program. No rational manager is going to put his company at a competitive disadvantage with respect to costs, prices, or earnings. In addition to other good reasons for this judgment, there is the strong probability that his employment would be terminated.

For some socially responsive policies and programs, however, the competitive cost constraint is not ordinarily a serious handicap. Policies and programs that assure equity in hiring and career advancement for members of minority groups and for women possess both of the favorable characteristics for unilateral action cited above. They can generate constructive and measurable results, and they can be administered so as to avoid short-term competitive cost disadvantages. And they also can contribute to long-term profits. The record on this is clear and should be beyond debate. The same favorable characteristics can often be found in programs for using and aiding minority suppliers and for investing in and providing managerial counsel for enterprises owned by members of minority groups. At least a few companies have even discovered that unilateral programs for limiting or re-

15

moving environmental contamination can be profitable. This is by no means commonly the case, of course, but it is simplistic to assume that the possibility does not exist.

A number of programs that represent significant contributions to social performance can be applied within the ongoing operations of one company. Often, indeed, they will be profitable. Removing specific policies and practices that impede progression through management ranks of qualified members of minority groups or women will enrich the total management resources of an organization and contribute to more effective performance. Improvements in product design that simplify or reduce maintenance, eliminate hazards, or give increased assurance of safety in use are positive contributions to social performance that also are likely to strengthen market position. Safe and healthy working conditions are likely to contribute to gains in productivity, hiring advantages in tight labor markets, improved employee morale, and reduced personnel turnover. A variety of acts of good community citizenship can yield a comparable variety of tangible and intangible short-term and long-term benefits.

On the other hand, there are obvious limits to what may be desirable or feasible for one organization to do on its own. Some type of cooperative or coordinated strategy is indicated in either of two situations. The first is encountered when a proposed program would have disadvantageous cost and profit results relative to competitors, without compensating gains of any sort. The second situation is encountered when a single-company program would make no significant contribution—even as an example to other business organizations—to the solution or amelioration of a social problem. The issue of substantial cost disadvantage is present in some environmental contamination situations in which one company's contribution to improved environmental hygiene may have an insignificant effect on a total-community problem. It may also be present in product safety situations, as in the automobile industry, where prevailing customer attitudes do not encourage the use of added safety as an advantageous marketing feature.

There is clear potential for conflict between the profit-making responsibilities of corporate managers, on one side, and their emotional response to the expression of social needs, on the other. Unless a publicly owned company earns at a level satisfactory to its stockholders—"satisfactory" earnings in this context may be roughly defined as comparable to those of other publicly owned companies in the same industry—its senior managers will be brought under severe pressure. The simplest and most effective short-run strategy to increase earnings is to cut costs. And the costs most eligible for cutting are those associated with activities not essential to current operations. This is, of course, a familiar course for eroding the long-run profit potential and competitive position of an organization. Confronting this irrefutable logic, a chief executive officer should and must avoid commitments to socially responsive programs that are likely to be competitively damaging.

This proposition does not assert that many such programs do not generate social gains possibly equal to or greater than the single-company investment in their support. It simply postulates that such programs should not be funded by single companies operating in a competitive environment.

A chief executive officer should therefore be interested in exploring possibilities for organizing business responses to social needs even when unilateral action by his company would be either economically disadvantageous or socially meaningless. His strategic choice is between (1) trying to encourage a cooperative or coordinated program among organizations whose collective action can be effective and (2) moving alone or with others to solicit and attempt to influence some type of governmental action.

Probably the most important reason for examining the feasibility of some type of coordinated business approach to selected social problems is that it provides an opportunity for private management to plan and act free from governmental constraint. This consideration is equally significant for issues important to companies in a single geographic area (such as air or water contamination). Obviously, there are important long-range social and political considerations connected with any cooperative strategy. Equally obviously, there are legal considerations.

The long-run interests of business in a reasonably open, flexible, and pluralistic society are better served when business organizations are perceived to adopt an activist posture toward society's problems and discontents than when they are perceived to behave negatively or with indifference. Managers who understand how the American democracy works in trying to ameliorate social ills and who know that social problems not resolved by private means will be attacked by public means recognize that the stereotype of the business leader as a defender of the status quo can be a dangerous weapon in the hands of critics of business institutions. It is a fair conclusion that if the private enterprise system is ever abandoned in the United States it will not be for its economic inadequacies, but rather because it does not vividly demonstrate an interest in helping to create a society that satisfies the needs and wants of a majority of its citizens.

Some issues, of course, cannot be handled cooperatively, either for legal reasons or because of the reluctance of corporate officers to join a common effort. In these circumstances it is desirable for business leaders who are sensitive to the potential effects of unsatisfied social pressures to move at an early stage to solicit and help to shape appropriate governmental action. Such a strategy may be distasteful to executives, who have good reason for preferring minimum governmental involvement in economic and social matters. The record clearly indicates, however, that a rooted negative attitude toward all kinds of governmental response to perceived public needs is a losing game for business.

The institutions of government at every level of a democratic society ultimately must be responsive to perceived public needs. Since these needs are rarely uniform among all segments of the population, the political process usually involves a complex interplay of conflicting interests through time. The typical evolving experience is one of advances and retreats, experiments and abandonments. But the basic trend is clear and there is every reason to anticipate its continuance.

The principal reason for encouraging a positive attitude by business leaders toward governmental action in the absence of a feasible private alternative is that, while some political response to social needs is inevitable, the standards and procedures of public action are not inevitable. There are many ways to bring about a cleaner environment. Some are better than others—cheaper, more effective, with more advantageous cost-benefit balances, with fewer undesirable side effects. There are many ways to make the automobile a safer means of transportation, and only some of them involve designing expensive changes or new equipment in vehicles. There are many ways to provide more and better public health services. In all such situations, rational choice among available alternatives requires an understanding of technological potentials and limitations, cost inputs related to benefit outputs, and administrative feasibilities and impediments. Politicians lack expertise in these matters. So do most of the leaders of interest groups, who typically combine an enthusiastic interest in social results with no more than meager competence in designing effective and efficient administrative machinery for attaining them.

In contrast to politicians, who generally understand the legislative process well and the administrative process poorly, business managers generally understand the administrative process well and the legislative process poorly. This contrast points to the great potential of managerial contributions to the emerging contract between society and business. To create an environment favorable to constructive management participation in the political process, managers must learn to buy their tickets of admission by establishing their credibility. The first requirement in doing this is to demonstrate an affirmative attitude toward social problem solving. The second is to develop a sophisticated understanding of the democratic political process and how to interact with it. Advice usually is not welcomed from individuals whose perceived strategy is to oppose any governmental action up to the point when it appears to be inevitable, and then to come forward with offers to help draft legislation or administrative orders. Such tactics cannot fail to arouse skepticism, distrust, or even hostility.

Implementing Social Performance within the Organization

The second big question facing the chief executive officer is how to assure that approved socially responsive policies and programs are implemented throughout his organization effectively and efficiently. While the general problem of implementation is not different from that met in implementing any traditional corporate program, there are some unique and practical problems related to social performance.

The first of these problems is the location of responsibility for formulating corporate policies and strategies bearing on social issues. Since a corporation's social performance is presently an important and visible part of its total public face and performance, a strong case can be made for lodging this assignment in the office of the chief executive or in someone reporting directly to this office. The case is reinforced by the fact that decisions about socially responsive policies and programs can powerfully influence revenues, costs, and other aspects of ongoing operations. Beyond this, outside observers and critics of corporate social performance identify the chief executive officer as primarily responsible for what is done or not done in this area. He may well be more visible, and in the public's mind more responsible, for corporate performance on social issues than he is for almost any other aspect of the business.

Centralization of policy and program formulation for social issues invites potential conflict with the pattern of delegated authority in multidivisional organizations or even in more simply structured organizations with several profit centers. Practically all socially responsive policies and programs have operational impact. Decisions taken at decentralized management positions may have serious consequences for the business as a whole. While there can be little doubt that the chief executive officer should be personally involved in policy and program decisions in this area, he must find ways to bring line operating managers into the decision process. They have essential knowledge about external pressures and opportunities, and equally essential knowledge about local operating implications of corporate decisions.

The comment suggests a second tough problem for the chief executive officer. In an organization that is beginning to take cognizance of social performance as a significant determinant of policies and programs, there are likely to be negative attitudes in middle-management ranks. Three specific attitudes can be anticipated: skepticism, indifference, and hostility. Some middle-level managers may doubt top management's commitment to socially responsive policies and programs. They may appraise the chief executive officer's statements of concern and intention as "front-office public relations," in the worst sense of that unforgiving phrase. Some middle managers may be insensitive and indifferent to the whole issue. They may believe that it is probably inevitable, for reasons of law or social pressure, that certain minimum actions will be taken. But they believe or hope that the burden of response to social demands and expectations will be carried out by specialized corporate staff officers, with little impact on operations. Finally, some managers may be hostile. They see the actual or potential impact on their own responsibilities, and they don't like it. They anticipate constraints on their ability to meet normal profit, cost, and productivity operating targets, and resulting threats to the advancement of their careers. In short, there is a conflict between near-term operating goals and long-term policy and performance goals, comparable to the conflict between operations and planning.

Chief executive officers who are concerned about social performance will have to recognize and take steps to deal with these negative attitudes. Positive motivation is needed. This can be provided only through a combination of (1) inclusion of specific social performance objectives in managers' responsibilities, (2) measurement of accomplishment against these objectives, and (3) visible use of measured accomplishment as one element in the organization's reward-and-penalty system. When managers see that their execution of socially responsible policies and programs is evaluated in promotion and compensation decisions, along with performance in meeting familar profit, cost, and productivity goals, they will believe and they will be motivated. For obvious and valid reasons middle managers concentrate their attention and skill on the accomplishment of performance objectives for which they know they are held responsible. They appraise responsibility in terms of two familiar criteria. The first is what is measured, and the second is what is rewarded.

This suggests another critical problem area for the chief executive officer. Traditional cost and financial control systems have not been designed to illuminate most of the resource management issues associated with socially responsive policies and programs. Relatively little is known about how to measure the social cost throwoffs of environmental pollution. Parallel to this, little is known about how to measure the social gains related to reduction of pollution. We are similarly handicapped in measuring costs and benefits in almost every other area in which elements of American society are pressing for business response. Without such knowledge, expressed in some kind of quantitative terms, however crude, business will be a long way from rationality in allocating resources to social programs and in appraising their contribution as quasi-revenues to compare with investment and expense.

Private business will not be allowed to delay social responses until some appropriate quantitative measures can be developed. In recent years some corporations have taken affirmative actions without precise knowledge of costs and benefits: reducing environmental contamination, opening up jobs and career paths for members of disadvantaged groups, ghetto investments, and assistance to minority business enterprises. A broader response to the needs and expectations of our changing society probably will not be generated, however, until corporate executives can take reasonable, if rough, sightings on costs and pay-backs. This will contribute to building the necessary confidence base for internal decisions about allocating money and personnel resources. It also will facilitate compiling a record that can be reported in meaningful and credible terms to the financial community, to shareholders, to employees, to customers, and to the general public.

The Chief Executive's Role in Formulating Public Policy

Probably the greatest challenge of all for the chief executive officer is to perceive and accept his responsibility for participating in the formulation of public policy. Business leaders have three reasons for being concerned about how they relate to and participate in public policy formulation where it bears on the satisfaction of social needs. The first is the probability that the survival of the business system may be threatened in a society bereft of confidence in business institutions. The second is the public's perception that actions of business have been directly responsible for some of the social discontent. The third reason is the likelihood that, in the absence of business participation in public policy formulation, critical clauses in the emerging social contract will be drafted by those who are ignorant about, or even contemptuous of, the enterprise system.

24

To retain the economic, social, and political advantages of the private enterprise system, we need a flexible modification of those elements in the system that either have contributed to extreme public disaffection and social injury or have failed to ameliorate the human and physical decay of urbanized, industrialized society. This adaptation is more likely to be effective and efficient if those who understand and value the enterprise system share in its redesign and are skilled in implementing their desire to participate.

Unless business leaders undertake this assignment, we are all going to be in trouble. There can surely be no greater economic and social danger than in permitting the terms of the new social contract to be drafted by either the small group of critics armed only with malevolence toward the enterprise system or the much larger group who are motivated by genuine concern for curing social ills but are handicapped by their ignorance of how to bring the resources and skills of the enterprise system to bear on creating constructive solutions while retaining the benefits of the system.

This is a challenge of massive proportions. To influence social change through political institutions, one has to understand how that change occurs. One has to understand the structure and behavior of social and political institutions. One has to be knowledgeable about the formal and informal channels through which influence and persuasion move, and about the opportunities and constraints that confront those who want to influence and persuade.

Interests, knowledge, and skills of this kind are not usually found among business leaders. There is a simple explanation for this deficiency. Business leaders have not depended on these talents in building their successful careers. They have not had occasion for acquiring valuable educational experiences in these areas and have not been selected for top-level assignments because of their possession of these assets. In the years ahead, however, possession of the skills required for effective performance of roles of public influence surely will attract increasing attention in the process of selecting managers for top-level responsibility.

The incentive for corporate leaders to share in exploring ways and means for removing cancerous growths in the society is classically selfish. Recognition is spreading that a continuance of these growths will be intolerable. Somehow they will be removed. An effort to ameliorate their effects is inevitable in a democracy. Uninformed solutions may be destructive of other valued constituent elements in our society, including the private enterprise system itself. Managers are equipped to contribute rational analysis and technical competence. Their interest in continuing the enterprise system coincides with the interest of other groups in continuing an open, healthy, adaptive society.

Social Responsibility or Social Performance

Confusion and hostility have been created in the business community by descriptions of the emerging social contract as an instrument that defines a new social responsibility for business. It is neither accurate nor constructive to portray a business role in terms of a social responsibility that is inconsistent with the long-run economic interests of the owners of resources in a private enterprise system. Such a responsibility should not be accepted by business leaders, nor will other interest groups permit business to accept it.

The central issue confronting management is one of social performance, not social responsibility. It develops from the fact that business organizations, notably the large corporations that are the administrative expression of the economics of resource use under advanced technology, are social as well as economic institutions. Their internal and external behavior exerts a massive impact on almost every aspect of social experience. It is therefore inevitable and proper that society should call for an accounting for corporate social performance and should propose new criteria for evaluating that performance.

The great test for managers will be their ability to understand this call, and to design constructive responses that will join social performance to economic performance in the context of the long-run interests of the owners of business. This requires a capability for controlled, creative adaptation to change. There is good reason to be at least moderately optimistic about the prospects for successful adaptation. Precisely this capability for controlled creative absorption of change has distinguished the private enterprise system in the industrialized democratic societies of the United States, Western Europe, and in recent years Japan.

Notes

1. *The Corporation in Transition: Redefining Its Social Charter* (Washington, D.C.: Chamber of Commerce of the United States, 1973), p. 23.

2. Reported in *The New York Times,* January 3, 1971.

3. *Social Responsibilities of Business Corporations,* a Statement on National Policy by the Research and Policy Committee of the Committee for Economic Development (New

York: Committee for Economic Development, 1971); *Measuring Business's Social Performance: The Corporate Social Audit,* by John J. Corson and George A. Steiner in collaboration with Robert C. Meehan (New York: Committee for Economic Development, 1974).

4.   In Neil H. Jacoby, *Corporate Power and Social Responsibility* (New York: Macmillan Publishing Co., 1973).

2

Concepts of Corporate Social Performance

Within the range of divergent views about the role and performance of business in its enveloping society are two areas of general agreement. The first is the belief that by the authority of both historical experience and specific legislation the business system in general and the corporation in particular are creations of the society and are enfranchised to function by the society. The second is the belief that although the business system and its constituent institutions are primarily oriented toward economic goals, the pursuit of economic goals inevitably generates a variety of social effects. These two beliefs have obvious linkages, since people who have favorable or adverse experiences with the economic and social effects of business operations may over time change their views about the business system and the terms of the franchise granted to business institutions.

Differing ideas about the appropriate role and performance of business take off from both areas of general agreement. At one end of the opinion range is the view that the sole and proper function of the business system is to produce economic goods in response to economic motivation. Within the system, managers of individual firms direct their efforts toward maximizing returns on invested capital, subject to judgments on acceptable risks and trade-offs between immediate and longer-term gains. Those who hold this view argue that economic performance was precisely society's objective in enfranchising business institutions. Any introduction of noneconomic considerations is seen as a triple perversion of the purpose behind the franchise (1) because business institutions were not created for noneconomic ends; (2) because business managers have no competence to achieve those ends; and (3) because investment of resources for noneconomic ends inevitably exerts an adverse influence on economic productivity and on overall economic and social health, and consequently cannot fail to weaken and ultimately destroy the business system, which is central to the survival of our democratic society.

At the other extreme is the view that the business system and its corporate institutions bear inescapable social responsibilities that are implicit in their enfranchisement and explicit in their performance. If these perceived social responsibilities are not fulfilled to a degree and in a manner generally satisfactory to prevailing public concepts, influential groups within the society will use the instruments of power available through the democratic process to compel fulfillment of social responsibilities through business institutions or in other ways.

Those who hold this view dismiss as false, deceptive, or trivial the thesis that the competences of business institutions and their managers uniquely qualify them to accomplish economic ends, and are misdirected, counterproductive, or even totally destructive when addressed to social ends. Skeptical of the willingness of managers voluntarily and in good faith to commit resources for what managers view as noneconomic ends, however, proponents of unqualified corporate social responsibility want social rather than business institutions to determine and administer standards for business performance, codes for business behavior, and procedures for measuring and controlling all business activities that have social impact. Like the economic purists at the other extreme, they point to the survival of our democratic society as the ultimate prize at stake.

Between these extremes is a range of philosophical and operational positions that reflect (1) differing value judgments with respect to voluntary and mandated—private and public—decision making, (2) differing assessments of costs and benefits along the continuum from voluntarism to authoritarianism, (3) differing concepts of the social value of economic gain and the economic value of social gain, (4) differing ideas about the feasibility of adapting existing institutions (notably the large corporation) to a new mission, (5) differing ideas about the extent to which those who are involved in the business system are qualified to participate in defining new standards for business performance, and (6) differing ideas about the nature of our democratic society and the sufficient conditions for its survival.

Part of this dispersion of views can be attributed to variant ideas about the content of social performance itself. On one side are those who believe that production of goods and services is not only a significant social function but also the only proper social function for business institutions. On the other side are those who believe that the social function of business encompasses the kinds and qualities of goods and services produced, the condi-

31

tions under which they are produced, the selection and treatment of the people involved in producing them, and the environmental impacts of the production process.

These are issues of great importance to all members of our society. They are even more significant for those charged with directing large corporations, who confront an environment undergoing severe turbulence along its several dimensions: economic, technological, social, and political. Managers cannot escape involvement in the contest of ideas. Either they participate in the contest and help to formulate the critical decisions that will be its outcome, or they, together with the business system in which they exercise commanding influence, will be the passive victims of others' decisions. It may be emotionally attractive to some managers to regard all proponents of change as witless dreamers or dangerous revolutionaries armed with concepts more potent than bombs. But it is surely not a winning strategy.

Statics and Dynamics of Social-Economic Linkages

One issue that emerges rather clearly from the conflict of opinion is that both enduring and transitory elements are involved in the debate. Indeed, a considerable share of the controversy can be attributed to disparate views about what is static and what is dynamic and about the appropriate weighting of the two elements in formulating value judgments.

The economic historian, for example, sees the American business system taking off from an initial period of resource exploitation and primitive industrialization in which society's needs and wants for basic economic goods far exceeded the supply capability of the business system. As manufacturing and marketing advanced in aggregate output and in efficiency of resource utilization, concepts of acceptability and adequacy in living standards also advanced (stimulated, in part, by improvements in mass communications). It is easy to understand why in such circumstances environmental spoliation was a topic of negligible interest.

Even in today's extraordinarily affluent society, the economically underprivileged and disadvantaged are intensely concerned about getting more and better goods and services and are only minimally interested in environmental hygiene. When the chips are really on the table as between job security and environmental improvement, jobs win. Popular concern about the quality of life comes into flower when popular concern about the GNP wanes—when the quantity of life is widely perceived to be reasonably provided for. On the world scene, it is in the countries that have attained an advanced stage of industrialization that powerful interest groups challenge the adequacy of the GNP calculus to define the good life. In countries still in early stages of economic growth, basic demands for shelter, food, and clothing are paramount, and concern about the social costs of industrialization is negligible. None of these disparities should be identified as examples of amorality or callousness. They are the result simply of a rational ordering of human priorities.

The shift in values that is reflected in today's changing concepts of the appropriate role and performance of business institutions is a shift in weighting of values, not an attempt to substitute one set of values for another. In a population in which demand outran supply, paramount social needs were indeed served by growth in economic output. It made no sense for most people to worry about a separable class of social needs, and, being sensible, they didn't worry. The GNP calculus was a valid measure of social as well as economic well-being. It is not a valid measure today. There was a time in our history when the critical economic and social need was to build energy resources by mining coal and pumping oil, without regard to the environmental effects of either activity. Today, the balance between energy availability and environmental impact is evaluated otherwise. If energy costs rise further and if energy availability is limited in the future, we may experience still a different evaluation of the trade-off between costs and benefits.

The business system has always served both economic and social ends. Until recently, economic ends were viewed as identical with social ends, and GNP measures were generally accepted as equally valid for assessing economic and social progress. Now, in what some have called a "postindustrial" phase of development, a distinction is being drawn between the economic and social performance of the business system and its institutions. We are beginning to recognize both economic and social consequences and trade-offs. This is not a development which in itself should be strange or alarming to managers. If the social majority is concerned about inequities experienced by members of minority groups in schools, restaurants, and transportation, it is natural and inevitable that the same concern should arise about inequities in employment and career opportunities. The thrust of women for equal rights in every part of their lives could not reasonably exclude their opportunities as workers, managers, and professionals—even, indeed, as religious leaders. It is not a conceptual outrage, however disturbing its economic implications, for a social majority to insist that business internalize production costs, such as air and water pollution, which the popular majorities of predecessor generations accepted as a fair burden for plant communities in return for the economic benefits generated by jobs and payrolls.

This does not mean that the effects of these attitude transformations should be accepted by business without opposition, or even that reformers' goals or methods are always in the public interest. Social improvements are seldom presented in terms that compel cost-benefit analysis, and it is easy to be enthusiastic about improvements unaccompanied by price tags.

Prevailing ideas about standards and priorities for corporate social performance clearly change through time. An inventory of ideas that occupy dominant positions and are widely endorsed today will probably be appraised as incomplete or in other ways off target in the mid-1980s. These changes occur for a variety of reasons. Some changes are the result of a long process of evolutionary development brought to climax by a charismatic activist leader (such as Martin Luther King, Jr., for black interests, or Ralph Nader for consumer interests), or the knitting together of scattered and weak local organizations into a coordinated and powerful national force (as in the environmental area). Some changes are set in motion by unanticipated events (such as the organization of the petroleum producers' cartel). Some come into being because of public revelation of activities long practiced in private obscurity (such as the recent flood of news stories about previously secret illegal or morally doubtful uses of corporate funds for political and commercial purposes).

Both the general phenomenon of broad changes in standards and priorities for corporate social performance and the character and timing of specific changes must claim an important position on managers' agenda. Management needs to anticipate the probable shape of things to come in the areas of national and industry economics, customer product and service preferences, and technologies relevant to the business; management has an equal need to examine probable developments in social expectations for business performance.

Social Responsibility or Social Performance?

Most managers, along with some economists and other observers of current pressures for changed patterns of business behavior, are disturbed and antagonized by references to "corporate social responsibility." This is not an unreasonable reaction. What is involved is not a matter of semantic style, but of intellectual substance. The phrase "corporate social responsibility" suggests a business obligation to deliver benefits to society beyond producing goods and services with the objective of maximizing return on invested capital, while operating in compliance with all applicable laws and government regulations. This suggestion is loaded with complex problems.

Who defines the bounds and specific content of the responsibility of a corporation to deliver benefits to society? Is the implementation of social responsibility a course of action determined by a corporation's chief executive officer, possibly in consultation with his board of directors? What about the effect of such action on costs, and therefore on profits and return on investment? How does a responsible manager mediate the conflicting claims among elements of the society whose objectives and priorities are not identical? Does a company's social responsibility extend to the amelioration of social ills not caused by its own actions, or even by the business system? Even these few questions are sufficient to indicate the slipperiness of the concept and its lack of operational content.

In spite of these intellectual brambles, managers are reluctant to abandon the idea of social responsiveness because they know there is something embedded in it that is real, important, and useful. Many corporations, as a result of management decision, do things that are beyond the traditional limits of their economic charters. They contribute to charities and to the support of organizations that deliver a variety of social services. They support the arts. They make gifts to colleges. Long before society mandated equal employment, some companies practiced it. Long before business morality became front-page news, some business leaders laid down codes of conduct for their organizations' relations with employees, customers, suppliers, and communities.

Behind these diverse practices can be found an equally diverse, yet curiously related, array of social views. At one end of the spectrum are managers who believe in their own and their organization's responsibility for the health and well-being of the enveloping and enfranchising society. Whether through a commitment to the tenets of institutionalized religion or through the inner guidance of individual morality and conscience, they truly believe that all men are brothers and they are their brothers' keepers. At the other end are managers who view the business corporation as an institution which, although formed for economic ends, cannot avoid affecting society by its actions and must continue to be acceptable to society if it is to retain its franchise. They take a long view of profit maximization, including in their profit calculation favorable feedback from all publics directly or indirectly influenced by their actions. They regret the inevitability of a certain amount of negative reaction to the perceived antisocial behavior of the business system, rather than positive reaction to the socially more enlightened and responsive behavior of their own companies.

Along the range between these extremes are managers who set courses for their organizations by balancing their perceptions of economic requirements (ultimately for their own survival) and social requirements (again, ultimately for their own survival). Because they apply personal value judgments to their economic and social perceptions, they reach different conclusions and reveal different patterns and levels of contributions and other corporate behavior vectors.

Much of the difficulty associated with these diverse concepts of corporate social responsibility can be avoided if we accept two propositions that are probably correct in general and easy to validate in particular instances. First, only a small number of managers are strongly guided by noneconomic motivations, and even this small group can survive only in situations of private, closely controlled ownership. Most managers cannot avoid the test of investors' appraisal of their performance. Second, public attitudes toward business are largely based on the degree of perceived congruity between actual business behavior and accepted standards of appropriate business behavior. The high level of general public approval of business reported by many social historians of the 1920s, for example, was encouraged by the high perceived congruence of actual behavior and accepted standards of appropriate behavior. For a variety of reasons, that congruence has been severely eroded in recent years, with results that are obvious to every manager.

The advantage of focusing on perceived congruence between actual business behavior and the accepted standards of appropriate business behavior is that the

concept of corporate social responsibility can then be re-
placed by the concept of corporate social performance.
Responsibility is outer-directed; performance is inner-
directed. Responsibility is under social control; performance is under management control. Managers of publicly-owned companies can decide what policies and
programs they will execute and can measure and evaluate their performance as perceived by significant
affected and observing publics. On the basis of these
evaluations, they can initiate, continue, modify, or abandon business policies and programs with important social
content. And they can make these decisions free from
concern about the legitimacy of forcing their concepts of
corporate morality on shareholders who believe they are
investing for economic gain, and not in philanthropy, or
public service, or the gratification of an unsullied conscience.

The test of corporate social performance then becomes
the familiar market test of long-run return to capital.
Investors' and observers' opinions, of course, will continue to differ about the profit potential of a company's
commitment to search, training, and developmental programs aimed at moving substantial numbers of women
and minorities into higher management ranks. Opinions
will also differ about investment in efforts to remove or
ameliorate urban blight and social distress in plant
communities, or in equipment designed to reduce environmental contamination. But so do investors' and observers' opinions differ about the long-run profit potential
of adopting new production technologies, entering new
markets, instituting new incentive compensation systems, or diversifying through acquisitions.

Corporate social performance, in short, is a decision
area that managers are as well equipped to handle as
corporate economic performance. In contrast, corporate

social responsibility throws up issues from which most managers wisely retreat. The fact that decisions about social performance usually involve evaluations of costs and benefits extending into future years is not an overwhelming handicap. Many economic investment decisions have comparably extended time horizons. Nor is the fact that decisions about social performance depend on value judgments—to some extent about costs and to a substantial extent about benefits—a persuasive reason for rejecting the assignment. To a greater extent than most managers seem willing to admit, the decisions they regard as central to their traditional responsibilities incorporate value judgments. Finally, the fact that decisions about social performance appear to take managers into areas where their competence is limited is simply a deficiency that the tide of events requires them to remove by the familiar remedies of analysis and developmental experience.

The Business of Business Is Business—Isn't It?

In the classic view of the role of business, social performance should never be a concern of management. The proper and only goal for management is profit maximization. To this uncompromising statement must, of course, be added two qualifications—in the long run, and within the law. As with other simple-seeming qualifications, these introduce complications which, in this period of social disturbance, may encourage consideration of the desirability of modifying the classic view.

The profit-maximizing postulate with its focus on economic performance, which has been articulated clearly and forcefully by Professor Milton Friedman, the distinguished Nobel laureate, is attractive on intellectual terms and appeals strongly to many corporate leaders. It was the prevailing philosophy within American business and its enveloping society throughout the nineteenth century and the first third of the twentieth century. The few querulous critics usually were barely discernible in the social mass, and their impact on business performance was generally limited to pressure for the enactment of legislation prescribing certain constraints on the conditions of employment for women and children. Antitrust and related legislation was thoroughly consistent with the prevailing view, indeed reinforced it by restraining the widely observed preference of managers for controlled as against competitive market conditions.

The inability of our industrialized, urbanized society to handle the harsh deprivations of economic depression in the 1930s generated for the first time serious public criticism of the thesis that the business system delivered social benefits by concentrating on economic ends. It revealed interlocks between economic malperformance and social pain, which few had previously discerned. Paradoxically, it was the economic affluence of the 1950s and 1960s, with its attendant opening of educational and career opportunities and the sighting of even more attractive possibilities, that created an environment that encouraged a second critical assault on business performance, starting with the proposition that there is more to the good life than is measured by the GNP calculus.

Were it not for these two attacks on perceived substantive deficiencies in business performance and their continuance and reinforcement in today's society, it would be hard to get a vigorous debate going on the soundness of the profit-maximizing postulate. Examined on its own terms, the proposition makes sense. It concentrates managers' attention on what they know and do best—how to produce and distribute goods and services. It frees them from concern about social and political issues that are loaded with unfamiliar and visibly complex elements. It provides the moral satisfaction derived from confidence that what they are doing is advantageous to owners, employees, and consumers.

The critical weakness in this "the business of business is business" concept is that today's social majority is clearly determined to change the rules of the game. The issue is not that the concept is wrong or inadequate. It was a thoroughly valid concept for a period when dominant public opinion (1) generally endorsed rising consumption of goods and services as the primary social goal, (2) largely ignored industrial pollution of air and water and despoliation of land and its resources, (3) was substantially indifferent to equity in employment and career progress, (4) accepted "let the buyer beware" as the standard for behavior in commercial transactions, (5) exhibited little concern about industrial safety and hygiene, and (6) generally believed that vigorous market competition would solve all consumer problems. Dominant public opinion no longer holds these views. In the new environment business managers are not permitted to focus their talent and energy solely on profit maximization. The concept is obsolete. It cannot reasonably be defended by describing its internal logic. The attack on the concept does not challenge its logic, but rather its relevance for a society that is drafting a new franchise for business and its institutions.

In this emerging situation, articulation of the economic advantages and philosophical purity of managerial concentration on traditional responsibilities, however elegantly expressed, contributes to mounting distrust of business and loss of credibility by its leaders. The final result of this line of defense, if not modified, will be a grievous wounding of the enterprise system by those who are not really its enemies and do not mean to damage it, but are simply intent, in their enthusiastic ignorance, on changing its behavior.

The indicated modifications are suggested by the two qualifications cited above: in the long run, and within the law. Since the social environment is as significant a determinant of business performance as the economic environment, sophisticated long-run profit-maximization strategies must be formulated with appropriate consideration for the opportunities and limitations for business in general and individual companies in particular that are likely to be created by the social environment. If this projection includes changed public expectations and demands related to business behavior, these new conditions for doing business become necessary elements in corporate planning. Similarly, if public pressures that are not satisfied by voluntary responses by the business community generate new legislation affecting business behavior (as has happened in recent years in environmental and plant hygiene, employment conditions, consumer protection, and other socially sensitive areas), profit maximization is inevitably subject to new rules and managers have good reason to be concerned about how they can participate in the legislative process. Introducing these two qualifications, however unattractive to purists, enlarges the meaning of "the business of business is business" in a way that calls for genuinely creative thinking by corporate leaders.

Should Business Help to Formulate Social Policy for Business?

A modified version of the profit-maximization concept acknowledges the social thrust for changes in business

43

behavior, but argues that managers lack competence and legitimacy to participate in the political process through which social needs and wants are implemented. This variation of "the business of business is business" does not defend the enterprise system against new legislative and administrative constraints. It admits the inevitability, even the desirability, of compelling corporations to internalize costs previously thrown out on society, to conform their behavior toward employees and customers to prevailing social norms, and in other ways to accommodate what they do and how they do it to society's requirements. But it postulates that it is society's job to define the rules of business performance, and that this is a process to which corporate managers should not contribute. In the same vein, it is critical of any effort by managers voluntarily to initiate cost-increasing modifications of company behavior (other than those likely to increase profitability) or to enter the political arena to debate the wisdom, standards, or techniques of change.

In its broadest expression this philosophy acknowledges that the conditions of life in our industrialized, urbanized society and the values shared by a majority of its citizens are significantly different from the conditions and values that prevailed in the nineteenth century and into the first half of the twentieth century. The social demand for a revised code of business behavior is not perceived as an aberration by those who hold this view. What is aberrant, they believe, is resistance by business leaders to the expressed requirements of contemporary society. All social institutions, including business institutions, must adapt to the evolving environment, or they will perish as surely as the brontosaurus. But the recommended adaptation is simply conformance with applicable laws, administrative regulations, and judicial rulings. The contribution of wisdom and perceptiveness is no more than recognition and acceptance of the inevitable. Society should determine what it needs from business and the manner of providing it. Business should accept those decisions and implement them.

For many managers this is a more uncomfortable concept than commitment to and defense of the pure profit orientation. In the latter situation, at least, they can with clear conscience identify the activist leaders of interest groups—passionate environmentalists, uncompromising agitators for instant equal rights, hard-line consumerists, enthusiasts for extended federal regulation and control—as ill-informed and dangerous socioeconomic romantics whose influence must be minimized and whose arguments must be debated. But to be counseled to accept the inevitability of fundamental changes in rules governing corporate behavior—with all their massive impacts on costs, decision procedures, risks, and liabilities—without undertaking either to defend the established system against such shocks or to draw on the knowledge and experience of successful practitioners to increase the effectiveness and efficiency of proposed innovations is hard advice for managers to live with.

The case for recommending that managers abstain from decisions affecting business-related social policies and programs rests, as noted above, on two propositions. The first is that managers bring no special competence to these issues. Nothing in their professional training and operating experience qualifies them to counsel on the needs of an evolving society, or on priorities among conflicting social interests, or on standards for social benefits and procedures for delivering benefits. The second proposition is that managers have no "right" to participate in the process through which social changes occur because they represent a franchised interest that is subservient to the determinations of the controlling society. Their efforts to intervene in the process of social change are therefore properly viewed as self-serving and fundamentally illegitimate. How can they be trusted to assist in solving social ills when, as many critics allege, they have been responsible for creating, or at least contributing to, the ills?

The case does not stand up under critical analysis. The society that is portrayed as afflicted by ills that require removal or amelioration is not a monolith. It is composed of a large number of special interest groups, some well defined and others vaguely articulated, some stable and others temporary, some mutually consistent and others conflicting. The great contribution of Western democracy to the quality of human existence is that it provides a political system within which special interest groups can articulate their concerns and compete for the satisfaction of their perceived wants. As many observers have pointed out, the system does not operate efficiently, and it does not necessarily result in justice and equity. It depends on popular consent, and this in turn requires accommodation by majorities to the needs of minorities.

These characteristics are exemplified in the array of current issues related to changing the business franchise. The claim is undoubtedly correct that most adult Americans now support the concept of equal employment and career opportunities. It is not at all clear, however, that the majority favor prompt correction of existing inequities that are the result of past practices. This requires quotas, reverse discrimination, and abrogation of contractual or accepted "rights," such as seniority in promotion or lay-off decisions. To all of these requirements there is moderate objection in general and fierce objection in specific instances. Opponents of air and water pollution have no trouble enlisting support for corrective legislation mandating high standards for environmental hygiene so long as most affected taxpayers and customers do not perceive the costs associated with the improvements. Popular enthusiasm wanes when the bills are confronted—in higher prices for products, energy shortages, and threatened plant closings and loss of jobs. Some of the dedicated supporters of women's rights have been surprised by the discovery of the rather large number of women who vote against specific enabling legislation. The list of examples could, of course, be extended.

In our pluralistic society, the interest of the owners of economic resources is as legitimate as any other interest. It does not have a dominant claim superior to other interests, but it is entitled to enter the debate and to participate in the political process. In large publicly-owned corporations, senior executives are the representatives of this interest. Their responsibility to manage invested resources for the benefit of shareholders surely encompasses a legitimate claim to participate in any political process as a result of which shareholders' interests may be adversely affected.

There is another and equally forceful reason for representatives of business to play an active role in the formulation of social policy affecting business. Much of the debate about the quality of life has been conducted in gross ignorance of cost-benefit trade-offs applicable to both specific quality standards (as in plant and environmental hygiene) and alternative means and schedules for upgrading performance toward approved standards. An interesting example of such cost-benefit trade-offs can be found in the public's concern about automobile-related deaths and injuries. In recent years, response to this concern has centered on increasing the safety features in automobile design—ability to absorb collision shock and the padding of interior surfaces—and on providing belt restraints and air bags. These changes add significantly to product cost and, in the case of belts and air bags, encounter considerable resistance to use.

We have only limited experience with two other approaches to reducing highway deaths and injuries, both of which would involve rather modest increases in economic costs (in the form of higher expenditures for police, court officials, and jails) but substantial social constraints. One of these approaches is lower speed limits, strictly enforced and with severe penalties for violators. The other is removal from the highways of drivers under the influence of alcohol, accompanied again by strict enforcement of the law (by random police roadblocks and on-the-spot testing of all drivers) and severe penalties for violators. An interesting examination could be made of the cost-benefit implications of various combinations of body design, occupant restraints, speed limitation, and discouragement of alcoholic drivers. Comparably interesting cost-benefit options with respect to both standards and processes can be identified in almost every area in which the social performance of the business system and its institutions has been criticized.

Experienced corporate managers have a responsibility for bringing such cost-benefit trade-offs and strategic alternatives into public view, and a capability for elevating the quality of public analysis of perceived social problems and the means for satisfying them. Whether managers will be allowed to convert this responsibility and capability into constructive participation depends largely on the public's perception of business attitudes. If business continues to be perceived as rigidly hostile to social change and unresponsive to the legitimate concerns of other interest groups—and there can be no doubt that business in general has contributed to this perception—it will not be welcomed or trusted in social policy formulation. The enlightened and constructive attitudes of some business leaders have not been articulated with sufficient clarity to the general public or sufficient persuasiveness to others in the business community to modify the negative image.

Is Profit Maximization Compatible with Improved Corporate Social Performance?

The key question that emerges from consideration of these concepts is whether profit maximization is compatible with improved business behavior. Will greater emphasis on corporate social performance, whether through business initiatives or governmental compulsion, weaken and possibly ultimately destroy the profit-seeking motivation of the private capitalist system, taking down the drain with it the energy and adaptability that have contributed so greatly to both economic and social progress? This is a critical question and it requires an answer.

One answer that clearly makes sense to some business leaders is that any departure from a commitment to profit maximizing is dangerous for the business system and equally dangerous for the enveloping society. Implicit in this answer is the idea that any concession to social performance which increases the cost of doing business is incompatible with a profit orientation. The idea is reflected in the adjective "nonproductive" that is frequently applied to investment in equipment and processes designed to reduce or eliminate noxious emissions that foul the air, effluents that degrade the quality of receiving bodies of water, and unhealthy conditions in the work place, as well as to investment in projects aimed at amelioration of urban blight and other community problems or even, at the extreme, to contributions to philanthropic, educational, and artistic organizations and activities.

The thrust of the argument is that such investment adds to costs without comparable gains in revenues. Over time, it is claimed, the inevitable result must be reduced profitability, inadequate funds for investing in economic growth, stagnant living standards, deterioration in the country's ability to compete in international markets, curtailment of employment and career opportunities, social unrest, loss of confidence in the United States among its worldwide allies and friends, impairment of the economic base of national security, and, further down the road, weakening of democratic institutions and disappearance of personal freedoms. If all this is indeed the inevitable result of investment to improve the quality of life beyond the goods-and-services range, it is a grim prospect, which no sensible person could favor.

Is this sequence inevitable? Will efforts to improve corporate social performance cripple the business system and inaugurate the decline of the American democracy?

In responding to these questions, it is relevant to observe that none of the supporters of improved corporate social performance have proposed that increased costs created by quality-of-life investments should be absorbed within existing profit margins. (There is, of course, gross popular overestimation of profit rates—an error to which ill-considered publicity releases and advertising by some corporations have contributed. But this is a different problem that should be dealt with on its own terms.) They assume that expenses connected with pollution control, occupational health and safety, and other gains in social performance will become part of the aggregate cost of doing business, which managers will try to recover through higher prices, thereby maintaining return on investment at a level that will continue to attract the capital required to replace worn-out and obsolete equipment and provide for growth. The rationale for higher product and service prices is that they reflect greater values to consumers, values that include a healthier, safer, more attractive environment; better protection of consumer interests; and other benefits.

The critical issue is, of course, whether this prospectus will be realized in practice. On the demand side of our market economy, consumers make purchase decisions that reflect judgments on cost-benefit balances, judgments that range from informed to intuitive. On the supply side, producers make pricing decisions that reflect judgments on cost-revenue balances, again ranging from informed to intuitive. The best guess about what will result from the interaction of these market forces is that the ability of business to maintain profitability by translating increased costs into increased prices will vary by industries and by companies within industries, exactly as in the past. No one can reasonably assure full across-the-board translation of costs into prices. The price elasticity of demand is predicted with more confidence in the economics classroom than in the marketplace. There will be a special problem for products in international marketing, where the implications of improved corporate social performance for U.S. exports and imports, in the aggregate and for individual companies, have not been even superficially examined by managers, union officials, consumer leaders, or social activists.

All these uncertainties strengthen the need for detailed, probing analysis of the specific individual-company advantages, costs, risks and feasibilities that are associated with joining social objectives to economic objectives in corporate plans and strategies. The same uncertainties strengthen the need for comparable evaluation of the implications for the business system as a whole. We do not confront an either/or situation, but one in which reasoned choices must be made. In some circumstances it will appear advantageous for a company to undertake initiatives on its own. In others, only concerted action by an industry or other industrial grouping may be feasible. In still other situations, the only possible course will be governmental action. Some demands of the proponents of improved quality of life will surely carry a price tag that most consumers will not accept, once they understand the cost-benefit trade-off. Individuals and whole communities will reject some demands when they face real choices, and examples of precisely this reaction have already occurred.

Responsible business leaders have an opportunity to demonstrate to critics, skeptics, and the uncommitted general public that their concern for the quantitative and qualitative aspects of the American society is equal to that of other members of the society. They cannot do this with an attitude of uncompromising negativism toward all proposed changes in the role and performance of business. Only as business is widely perceived to be committed to constructive participation in the process of defining opportunities and feasibility limits will it rebuild its seriously weakened credibility. The business response to this opportunity can be an initiative that will convert the present state of contending philosophies into the greatest opportunity that has ever existed for constructive, socially peaceful evolution in fundamental relationships in a postindustrial society. It can also be a retrograde, ultimately destructive effort to defend a position that is no longer defensible, to protect obsolescence against creative evolution.

3

Offensive and Defensive Strategies

THE legitimacy of the established business system is now directly challenged. Critics complain about inadequacies in its economic and social performance, its sluggish response to society's evolving wants and needs, and its stubborn opposition to proposals for changing the terms of its franchise. Those who value the business system's contributions point to the critics' ill-conceived, superficial, even dangerous ideas for improving the system's social performance. They are concerned about the critics' indifference to the economic and social costs associated with certain desired benefits. They fear the critics' ignorance of the absolute dependence of new investment for capital replacement and growth on adequate profitability, and their insensitivity to the social benefits created by the dynamism inherent in relatively unfettered private enterprise. The content of charges and responses is as much emotional as it is intellectual. This does not, of course, reduce the seriousness of the debate

53

or lighten the critical economic and social commitments inherent in actions taken and proposed.

In this complex situation, those with a stake in existing business institutions have good reason to think hard and carefully about the institutions' future in a society squeezed by conflicting pressures for continuity and change. On one side, stubborn resistance to all proposals to modify business behavior and its institutional arrangements weakens public confidence in business leaders and encourages special interest groups to use the political process to compel acceptance of their preferred reforms. On the other side, some of the proposed changes are clearly impossible of attainment. Some changes appear to involve economic or social costs that would not be accepted by the general public. Some changes would destroy or dangerously weaken the competitive position of plants or companies, with consequent loss of employment and depletion of host communities' economic nourishment. Some would present difficult technical or administrative problems that need to be resolved before commitments are made. Some would raise complex options within the cost-benefit or end-means calculus that require comprehensive analysis to identify trade-offs, opportunity costs, and system relationships. In short, a rigid commitment to change is as dangerous as a rigid commitment against change.

There can be no workable resolution of this conflict that will retain the economic and social benefits of the existing business system and also facilitate its accommodation to society's evolving needs and wants unless business leaders commit themselves to an activist strategy that is realistic, flexible, adaptive, and pluralistic. It must be realistic in recognizing that powerful forces in our society are demanding, and beyond question will get, some changes in the role and performance of the business system and business institutions. It must be equally realistic in recognizing that the changes that occur need not be those currently recommended by the most aggressive interest groups. It must be flexible in distinguishing among the variety of situations in which economic and social interests are inextricably involved. These situations present a range of cost-benefit relationships that will require a comparable range of accommodations, adjustments, and compromises. The strategy must be adaptive in responding to evolving social values, prepared in appropriate circumstances to design new concepts and methods in business-consumer, business-community, business-government, and business-public relationships. It must be pluralistic in its readiness in some circumstances to defend the status quo and rebut change; in other circumstances to anticipate public demands and initiate changes; in its readiness to accept new goals and standards for corporate social performance when appropriate, while working to demonstrate the infeasibility of proposed methods for achieving them and recommend alternative approaches to the desired goals; and, in still other circumstances, in its readiness to participate aggressively in the democratic political process.

This approach to accommodation of business institutions to a changing society is neither ideological nor dogmatic. It is an approach that evaluates each element of the changing environment in terms of both economic and social costs and benefits. Implementation of this approach will encourage corporate leaders to develop multiple strategies. Some strategies will reflect initiatives for change beyond current proposals of interest groups. Some strategies will comply with and support ideas generated outside the business community. Some will accept proposed social objectives, while rejecting proposed ways of accomplishing them and urging alternative procedures likely to achieve desired results more effectively and efficiently. Some will vigorously defend existing institutional arrangements and practices. Whether a given strategy is offensive or defensive in character, it is important that business leaders commit themselves to active participation in the process of reviewing and revising the business franchise. Such a role will fully reflect their responsibility to shareholders to maximize the long-run return on investment in a new social environment. If business leaders perform this role well, they will go far toward accommodating social and economic objectives within a common corporate planning process, and, on the national scene, equally far toward removing the invidious distinction between private interest and public interest.

Offensive Strategies: Characteristics, Opportunities, and Risks

Offensive strategies available to management in responding to challenges to improve corporate social performance share certain common characteristics. First, corporate leaders who design such strategies have an open attitude toward social change. They understand and are comfortable with the idea that an essential condition of survival for all human systems and institutions is their capacity for selective adaptation to a changing environment. Second, the range of strategies suggests that both the nature and the process of possible business responses to a changing environment are richly varied in relation to a company's market position, resources, technology, and other considerations. Third, the strategies are not confined to simple reactions to expressed criticism and challenge. They include actions designed in anticipation of pressures for change, actions that take control of issues by preemption of the leadership position, and actions that earn for business the right to participate with other groups in formulating remedial policies and programs. Fourth, offensive strategies are influenced by cost-benefit analyses. Finally, these strategies include public education and communication as important elements in the strategic mix. It is not only what business does that counts, but how broadly and clearly its actions and motives are perceived and understood.

The central management philosophy expressed in all these characteristics is the commitment to an activist posture for business in its relations with the social and political environment. The range of offensive strategies encompasses (1) strategies that identify potential causes of discontent with corporate behavior and remove them or reduce their significance by anticipatory initiatives; (2) strategies that respond directly to criticism by correcting or modifying the target of criticism; (3) strategies that, while accepting the necessity or inevitability of government action to compel specific social performance, develop and promote what are likely to be effective and efficient regulatory policies and procedures; (4) strategies that identify well-intentioned but ill-designed governmental regulatory programs and urge adoption of more effective and efficient programs; and (5) strategies that direct public attention to inconsistencies or contradictions among government objectives for improved social performance, and recommend better-coordinated alternatives. Many of these strategies are mutually consistent, even reinforcing, and can be deployed in combination.

Managers who are sensitive to the desirability of coordinated planning for economic and social objectives will find it advantageous continually to scan the social environment and to project trends and developments into their long-range planning process, together with economic, competitive, technological, and market projections. The first objective of such an early warning system should be to identify opportunities for taking constructive initiatives to correct unsatisfactory corporate social behavior wherever remedial action is feasible, within economic, technological, or other constraints. Long before the enactment of legislation mandating fair employment practices, for example, it would have been feasible and advantageous for individual organizations to institute policies assuring nondiscriminatory hiring and career experiences for women and members of minority groups. Any corporation taking such a voluntary initiative at an early stage would have gained access to a valuable pool of talent ahead of its competitors. If most large business and other organizations had behaved in this way during the decades when the growing public concern about employment and career discrimination was clearly visible and when the inevitability of corrective legislation was predicted by many observers, the pressure for legislation would have diminished and current problems in operating under rigidly restrictive legislation might never have arisen.

Imaginative action by an individual company to identify at an early stage consumer dissatisfaction with common marketing policies and practices and make appropriate and feasible corrections and improvements in its own policies and practices can generate significant competitive advantages. If such constructive initiatives had been taken voluntarily by most large corporations in the 1950s and 1960s—in such familiar areas of consumer concern as meaningful description of product content, nutrition, terms of sale, guarantees, repair services, product safety, financing terms, advertising claims, and other issues familiar to all who have observed the rising tide of organized consumer discontent—much of the unnecessarily burdensome, unduly restrictive, clumsily designed protective legislation might not have been enacted. In addition, corporate executives and trade associations would enjoy the public credibility and confidence required to be allowed to participate in drafting legislation and engineering administrative machinery to control the marketing malpractices of marginal firms.

The critical issue in areas of public concern with corporate behavior is not to propose management actions that are competitively disadvantageous because they increase costs without compensating additions to revenues. Rather, it is to encourage imaginative exploration of ways and means of profiting from constructive early responses to changes in public attitudes toward business behavior. The benefit for the individual company may develop in one or more of the following ways. First and most obviously, the actions may assist in winning a larger market share and more sales as a result of increased consumer benefit or reduced dissatisfaction. This is the likely outcome of changes in the product-service-marketing mix that satisfy emerging consumer needs better than competitors' offerings and practices. Second, they may contribute to improvements in productivity that reflect more effective resource utilization, lower employee turnover, enhanced employee morale, reduced training costs, and related positive developments. These are some of the likely benefits from equal employment and career policies and practices. Third, they may facilitate conversion of industrial wastes into commercial products and services. This is a possible outcome of investment aimed at discovering more socially acceptable technologies. Beyond these directly accountable gains are potential indirect benefits of enhanced employee, customer, and community goodwill; local and national recognition and leadership status; and opportunities to participate in and constructively influence legislative and regulatory processes at the formative stage.

Imaginative initiatives by a few companies, which yield both immediate and longer-term competitive advantages, will not prevent adverse public assessments of the general level of business social performance, restore the general credibility of business leaders, or discourage or modify legislative and regulatory pressures by interest groups. Only fundamental changes in the pattern of social performance of most large corporations will alter such general attitudes toward the business system. Only constructive initiatives by substantially all the leading firms in an industry will persuade those who are legitimately critical of the quality of that industry's social performance to revise their judgment. Rewards for the innovative minority will be direct and indirect, short-term and long-term gains in comparative performance versus less enlightened competitors. These are not trivial rewards, but it is important to understand that the business system in general will be evaluated in terms of its perceived general performance. This is the justification for encouraging educational and counseling programs sponsored by broad-based organizations such as the Chamber of Commerce of the United States and trade and professional associations.

Nothing in the preceding discussion is intended to recommend initiatives by a company's management to accommodate any aspect of its social performance to perceived public criticism when the result of such action would adversely affect its economic performance or its competitive position. Maximum long-term return to shareholders must continue to be the dominant objective for corporate management. Any breach of this guiding principle—as in additions to costs that erode a company's competitive performance—should only be at the behest of public authority expressed through proper legislative, executive, or judicial action. There are many circumstances, however—a number of which are cited in the discussion above—in which corporate initiatives to make social performance consonant with public wants and expectations can improve a company's competitive position, or at least can be taken without significant adverse effect on immediate or projected profitability. Such initiatives are advantageous for the initiating firm. If taken by many firms, they are advantageous for the business system as a whole.

This line of reasoning favoring aggressive corporate strategies in an environment of changing social attitudes toward corporate performance can be extended to support active participation by business management in all aspects of the political process, particularly those related to legislative or regulatory decisions affecting corporate social performance. Whenever initiatives by a single company are not feasible, because of their unacceptable adverse effects on the company's competitive position, in an environment in which there is considerable public dissatisfaction with some aspect of business performance or failure to perform, it is still advantageous for its managers to play an activist role in developing a governmental solution to the problem. In a democratic society popular discontent inevitably will seek, and ultimately will get, governmental relief. The relief recommended by the leaders of special interest groups may have extremely damaging consequences for business, and therefore for those associated with business as owners, employees, customers, or host communities. The recommended relief may be less effective than an alternative solution, may be needlessly wasteful in resource utilization, or may conflict with other governmental objectives and programs.

The significance of the strategic issue is suggested by a few examples from recent history. Excessive and uninformed zeal in pursuing the attractive goal of unpolluted air and water leads to sharply increased product and energy costs and prices, which are likely to cause general inflation, curtailed production, loss of jobs, erosion of some communities' economic base, and other economic and social disruptions. Excessive and uninformed zeal in pursuing the attractive goal of preventing gross destruction of the landscape by strip mining is likely to result in critical shortages of energy, with attendant economic and social costs that would be recognized as unacceptable even by some of the enthusiastic opponents of strip mining. Excessive and uninformed zeal in bringing about immediate equality of personnel policies and practices for all previously disadvantaged groups is likely to release dangerously divisive forces in our society. Excessive and uninformed zeal in pursuing the attractive goal of products safe enough to be foolproof in the hands of fools is likely to raise product costs and prices to levels that will sharply shrink their markets.

The message communicated by these examples is not trivial. Not only the interest of the business system and its institutions but also the interest of our society as a whole in rational allocation of resources will be assisted if business managers participate in the decision process. Since resource allocation decisions inevitably are influenced by the disparate values of special interest groups, the decisions will be developed through the interplay of power confrontations and coalitions acting on and within political institutions and procedures. The more relevant and specific the information on economic and social costs and benefits that can be introduced into the decision process, the better for the real interest of all who must live with its results. Business managers can make important informational contributions to the decision process. To win trust and acceptance for their contributions, however, they must be accepted as credible collaborators. If they are generally perceived as hostile to all proposals for changes in the role and performance of business institutions, they will be automatically identified as adversaries. They will not be trusted, and their recommendations will not be accepted.

Defensive Strategies: Characteristics, Opportunities, and Risks

It is equally important for corporate leaders to develop defensive strategies designed to protect the business system and its institutions against ignorant or even hostile critics and against proposals for change that would damage the system's ability to continue to deliver its unique economic and associated social contributions. The enterprise machine is in many ways extraordinarily tough and resilient, but has vulnerable points where it can be easily disabled. Recent history has demonstrated that two of the most sensitive characteristics of the business system are its inability to absorb sudden cost overloads and its vulnerability to inflationary pressures that tend to be self-reinforcing and resistant to damping. It is therefore critically important to recognize that many well-intentioned but ill-considered ideas for compelling business suddenly to internalize costs previously disseminated through the external society can inflict severe and possible irreparable damage.

The environmental pollution, product safety, and production process areas offer many examples of special interest groups' demands to transfer costs in this manner. They are proposed without adequate consideration of desirable time horizons, inflationary potential, interfirm or interindustry dislocations, or the affected employee groups' or general public's willingness to accept costs in order to enjoy related benefits. A naive enthusiasm for reform, however desirable the reform may be in concept, can be an intolerably dangerous force if turned loose in a dynamic socioeconomic system in which institutional and market relationships have attained at least temporary equilibrium. A new set of viable accommodations may be a long time in development, and the intervening conditions are likely to be chaotic.

Individual firms and the system as a whole are also vulnerable to externally mandated changes that demand sudden shifts in the political balance among interest groups with stabilized intrafirm organizational relationships. Adjustments that can be absorbed if phased in over an extended period of time are likely to be fiercely resisted if forced on people at a faster pace than they find comfortable. Such resistance can become truly venomous if the effect of the change is not simply mandatory accommodation to unfamiliar relationships but is perceived as directly destructive of established powers, rights, and privileges. Instant and compensatory correction of long-continued discriminatory employment practices has spawned predictable counterproductive backlash effects. The unarguable fact that the discriminatory practices violate all norms of human decency and are grossly inconsistent with a central tenet of American democracy does not usually prevail over widely shared feelings of resentment about loss or curtailment of perceived rights. This is deplorable behavior with tragic consequences for many who have suffered disadvantages from which they should long since have been released. Yet it remains true that a time-phased program that permits a gradual adjustment to a new pattern is likely to achieve greater progress toward the desired goal than radical, immediate change. This is not an easy lesson for dedicated reformers to learn and apply.

The most effective way to develop successful defensive strategies against ill-considered or dangerous proposals for changing corporate social performance is to combine rejection of defective recommendations with positive approaches to solving underlying problems. A principal reason for the loss of credibility so often deplored by business leaders is the general public's perception that as a class they throw up "knee-jerk" defenses of the status quo, are insensitive or indifferent to social issues that seriously disturb large numbers of people, and are not interested in examining alternatives to the proposals they reject. This perception is strengthened whenever business criticism of reformist recommendations is expressed in narrow terms that ignore legitimate discontent while concentrating on deficiencies in reformist recommendations. It is also strengthened when business fails to take advantage of opportunities to join forces with other groups in our society whose interests would be adversely affected by the proposed reform.

Examples abound in recent history of failures by corporations and trade groups to understand the danger of unilateral negativism, and the inevitable erosion of public confidence in business leaders whose professions of commitment to the philosophy of competitive markets are perceived as inconsistent with their self-serving opposition to specific proposed changes in market processes. Senior executives of companies in regulated industries who attack proposals to simplify and reduce the regulatory machinery on the ground that more competition would "destroy the industry" sacrifice their own credibility and nibble at the credibility of all business leaders. Public confidence in the good faith of leaders of energy companies is weakened when some of those leaders attack proposed measures to protect the environment or assure public safety without acknowledging that there are genuine underlying problems for which workable solutions must be developed. Thoroughly justifiable business criticism of gross deficiencies in, and maleficent effects of, our patchwork welfare structure generates broad distrust when not accompanied by recognition of grievous distress and massive human waste in a generally affluent society and by a demonstrated willingness to participate in designing better solutions than those now in place. Business leaders' professions of concern for consumer interests are not generally trusted when efforts to protect those interests come under business attack as destructive of the competitive market system and when business spokesmen deny the legitimacy of consumers' complaints and the need for remedial action.

Business has a right, even an obligation, to criticize regulatory proposals that are unnecessary, that would create unreasonable restrictions on economic or social freedoms, that would be ineffective or inefficient in accomplishing desired economic or social goals, that would create administrative machinery and related burdens disproportionate to targeted benefits, or that would generate dangerous economic or social side effects. This criticism should be articulated vigorously. Nothing in these pages is intended to recommend restraint of any kind on the forthright expression of individual-company, industry, or general business views in opposition to needless, faulty, or dangerous proposals to correct alleged social malperformance by part or all of the business community. Indeed, business leaders are most likely to be listened to with attention and respect when they present their views in public frankly and in specific terms, even when these views challenge those of activist leaders who claim to represent "the public interest." There has been an insufficiency, rather than an excess, of informed criticism by senior corporate managers.

The real challenge is to combine criticism of incompetent proposals for changing the social performance of business with persuasive demonstration of concern about significant public issues and desire to participate in solving social problems. The absence of this combination has been a principal cause of the loss of credibility so often deplored by business leaders. Inadvertently, they portray themselves and the organizations they direct as adversaries of the public interest. This perceived posture is strategically dangerous for the enterprise system. If perception were reality, it would be disastrous. There can be no healthy future for business in a society that distrusts business institutions and their leaders and turns to other interest groups for solutions to broad social problems and remedies for the causes of public dissatisfaction.

Designing a Set of Strategies for the Individual Company

All large companies are involved in such complex interrelations with the social and political environment that no single strategy can be optimal for all issues. Analysis may indicate the desirability of pursuing offensive strategies in dealing with some issues, defensive strategies in dealing with other issues, and even on occasion adopting a neutral posture. For example, a particular corporate management in its unique circumstances may find it advantageous to take aggressive initiatives in opening managerial and professional career paths for women and blacks; to comply only when and as necessary with regulatory requirements for costly nonproductive investments to accomplish noise abatement in its plants; to seek opportunities to recommend and justify before Congressional committees and other government agencies technical specifications and administrative machinery for pollution control; to encourage and participate with broad-based business associations in formulating and publicizing proposals for innovative approaches to national welfare problems; to oppose vigorously special interest groups' uneconomic solutions to problems of unsatisfactory product performance; to seek coalitions with other companies in organizing voluntary responses to public discontent with aspects of their common behavior; to seek other coalitions with nonbusiness interest groups that share a common concern about community problems; and to design and implement its own code of ethics. There is no dissonance among these strategies.

Multiple decision criteria are essential analytical tools for developing rational management judgments about what to do and how to do it in each of such a formidable array of problem areas. The primary decision criterion should be the anticipated effect of any specific action or inaction on profits, both short-term and through an extended planning period. This is, of course, not a simple determination, since any action or failure to act is likely to affect revenues and costs, directly and indirectly, absolutely and relative to competitors. The context in which this test is applied should be an assessment of the opportunity for the individual company to take independent action that is feasible in relation to available resources, promises to accomplish significant and identifiable results, and holds out the prospect of generating a favorable long-term surplus of benefits over costs. Examples of areas in which the application of this profit criterion may lead to a decision to take positive action include implementation of nondiscriminatory personnel policies (including programs designed to remedy a legacy of prior discrimination); implementation of programs to reduce or halt environmental contamination and to improve safety and hygiene of the work place; and a variety of actions aimed at protecting consumer interests ranging through product information (advertising, sales promotion, public relations), terms of sale, product performance, product servicing, and effects of product use.

A second decision criterion should be the probability of externally mandated action as a result of legislative or regulatory developments, together with the economic implications of complying or failing to comply with the mandate. Here the relevant concerns are likely to cluster around the effects of mandated action on intraindustry and interindustry (and, for a growing number of industries, international) competitive relationships; the state of the art of applicable technology and administrative systems; the time period within which compliance is likely to be required; opportunities for successfully opposing, modifying, or delaying governmental action; chances for organizing effective coalitions with industry or other interest groups; and the availability of alternative solutions to the perceived problem to which the mandated action is addressed. Examples of areas often within the scope of this criterion include, in addition to many of those cited above in connection with the profitability test, significant changes in product design or performance (as in automobile safety, pollution, and fuel consumption); energy production and conservation; trade practices; corporate governance (as in federal chartering and the responsibilities and structure of corporate boards); and adjustment of the boundaries between the public and private sectors.

A third decision criterion should be the intensity of existing and projected public distrust or disapproval of business performance and behavior, whether directed at a specific firm, the industry of which it is a part, or the local or national business community. Widespread negative attitudes may be the result of ignorance or misunderstanding, as well as of accurate perception. Whatever the cause, general public disaffection weakens the society's commitment to the enterprise system, destroys confidence in business institutions and their leaders, and creates opportunities for activist reformers to exploit the pervasive discontent through radical revisions of political and social institutions. Examples of areas sensitive to this criterion include local, regional, or national economic distress and attendant social unrest; perceived business posture opposed to perceived public interest; perceived business violations of accepted standards of morality; and perceived discontinuities between business philosophy and business practice (as in commitment to competition while resisting proposals to relax or remove regulatory controls). The fundamental issue here is, in effect, the role and responsibility of business as a constituent element of the local or national community when the community's economic or social integrity is under severe pressure.

A fourth decision criterion should be the perception of opportunities for constructive initiatives by the company acting alone or in concert with others to contribute to the amelioration or solution of local, regional, and national economic and social problems. Positive demonstrations of good citizenship help to build respect for the business community and restore some of the lost credibility that is so often deplored by business leaders. Examples of areas deserving imaginative examination include temporary loan of qualified managers to local, state, and national government and not-for-profit institutions, particularly for assignments to improve information and decision systems and resource utilization; and formulation and recommendation of policies and programs designed to accomplish technological, economic, and social objectives more effectively and efficiently than existing or alternative approaches (as in pollution control, energy conservation, and welfare programs).

Selecting an appropriate mix of strategies—offensive, defensive, and neutral—clearly requires a sophisticated understanding of the impact and process of social change, an ability to relate social performance ends and means to economic performance ends and means, and a high level of communication skills in persuasively articulating strategic positions to various publics. These are demanding requirements, particularly in the context of the novelty of their appearance in the traditional managerial world and the inexperience of most managers in dealing with such issues. Evolving social dynamics suggest, however, that business leaders will not have the luxury of choosing to avoid the bramble of difficulties described above. Either they will organize to apply a high order of rational analysis to the determination of corporate strategies at the business-society interface, or they will have to manage under rules determined by nonbusiness interests. It is hard to see any advantage for the business community in the latter outcome. The real question is how to develop a set of strategies that will accommodate the mutual needs and interests of private business and the encompassing society.

The critical arena is the planning function. This is where ends and means, objectives and resources, are evaluated comprehensively and in detail. And this is also where social performance options must be examined, their economic implications identified and evaluated, and the limits of opportunity and feasibility determined. Strategic planning has progressed in substantially all large and many medium-sized firms in the last two decades from a rather primitive state to a formal activity that is respected as a management tool and applied with a fair degree of sophistication. With only a few exceptions, however, planning in most companies has been substantially limited to technological and economic ends and means. There is only superficial, if any, consideration of trends and forces in the social environment.

Most very large corporations now have an in-house professional economic resource principally assigned to industry and market analysis, supplemented by outside economic forecasting services. Other companies make regular use of outside services, often aided for specific assignments by independent consultants. Moreover, all managers at senior and middle levels are familiar with economic analysis and use it readily in strategic planning. On the other hand, few organizations presently possess or engage comparable professional competence in describing, interpreting, and forecasting social trends and attitudes, and in identifying through such analyses opportunities and threats in specific industry environments. In addition, few managers have the training or experience essential for dealing confidently with social materials. This professional and managerial gap must be filled with relevant knowledge and familiarity with its use as a foundation for strategic thinking of the kind described in this chapter.

Fortunately, the current need is greater for managerial understanding of the evolving social environment and for identifying its actual and potential impact on the business system than for suddenly introducing into business organizations professional expertise in charting and measuring social trends. The principal environmental thrusts and pressures are out in the open. What is generally lacking is a disposition to deal with them as continuing and powerful determinants of business performance, which also are, within broad limits, open to influence by knowledgeable business leaders.

There is a related need for a higher level of expository and negotiating skills than is now commonly found in corporate executive ranks in working with government officials and interest group leaders, and in articulating corporate policies and positions to public audiences. As this need is recognized, it can be confidently anticipated that a criterion of growing significance in selecting managers for senior positions will be their demonstrated possession of these skills.

4

Strategic Planning for Economic and Social Performance

THE uses of strategic planning as an administrative tool are well understood by managers of practically all large, most medium-size, and even many small corporations. Planning systems and plans are becoming increasingly sophisticated. The planning process is spreading through organizations from the corporate level to divisions, departments, and profit centers. With growing frequency, plans are linked to operations through incorporation of short-term increments of multiyear programs in annual operating budgets. The influence of this entire development on management attitudes, behavior, and performance is reinforced by periodic auditing of managers' achievement of planning objectives and reflection of these measurements in the reward-penalty discipline.

Long-term evaluations of opportunities and threats in the external environment and of internal-resource strengths and weaknesses are reflected in strategy formulation. Generated through a formal planning system and approved by senior management, strategies exert a powerful influence over major resource commitments and fundamental business policies. Investments and programs that are consistent with and supportive of an approved strategic plan command the attention of managers throughout the organization. Whatever is perceived as deviating from or likely to interfere with the plan is rejected or bypassed even if sponsored by high authority or recommended by its own apparent legitimacy. What is not included in the plan is not likely to be taken seriously by operating executives, particularly if the program or policy is perceived to threaten a negative impact on planned revenues, costs, profits, and return on investment, or on prevailing management attitudes, employee morale, or union relationships.

Both the literature on planning and informal surveys of business practice suggest that economic, market, and technological considerations are dominant in strategic planning. In only a few corporations do societal issues appear to exercise a significant influence. This is the principal reason why in many well-managed companies an extraordinarily flexible adaptation to economic, market, and technological threats and opportunities is so often accompanied by inertia in responding to changes in the public's expectations for corporate social performance.

This inertia is sometimes expressed in the form of unreasoning opposition to social change. There is a rather widespread management disposition to challenge social pressures as if they aimed at destroying the very foundations of the private enterprise system. Critics of even peripheral aspects of corporate performance are often accused of being enemies of the system, blind to its enormous vitality that has contributed so greatly to rising living standards. In return, this negative attitude is perceived by the critics as a rigid hostility to any accommodation to a variety of public dissatisfactions with the behavior of business, and as an unwillingness to recognize that corporations in our industrialized society are social as well as economic institutions.

This experience supports the conclusion that the only way to give effective expression to the social role of business institutions is to incorporate social performance considerations within the formal corporate strategic planning system. As long as issues related to social performance remain outside a company's planning system, they are unlikely to engage the sustained attention of senior managers. Under these conditions, specific socially responsive policies and actions may be perceived by line operating managers as impediments to their accomplishment of the objectives on which they believe their careers depend. At both levels, therefore, relationships and trade-offs among economic and social considerations lack the thorough analysis they require.

Adherence to this pattern of behavior encourages a growing share of the public to conclude that business institutions will not voluntarily serve important societal needs, that they must be compelled by law and regulation to conform to the public will. From such a development can come only ill-considered legislation and regulation and a consequent erosion of business flexibility and dynamism. It is a sad observation that this resistance to social change is totally at variance with the imaginative vitality with which entrepreneurial managers are accustomed to address economic, market, and technological developments.

Problems in Bringing Social Issues into the Planning Process

Introducing social considerations into the planning process is not easy. It presents three problems. The first problem is conceptual: persuading senior managers to feel comfortable with the idea that corporate social performance can be integrated with economic performance in formulating strategic objectives. Little in the education and experience of most members of the current generation of senior executives has prepared them to handle this concept. The sticky issue is not insensitivity to public criticism of certain aspects of corporate behavior. No business leader today can be unaware of the scope and content of the current unhappiness. The real difficulty is skepticism about the proposition that economic and social performance can be evaluated within a common set of cost-benefit calculations.

The fact that a few top officers of major corporations have publicly asserted the necessity and feasibility of such coordinated analysis has given the concept a degree of legitimacy. But most of their peers have not been persuaded that it can be made operational. The case for setting skepticism aside is clear and forceful, however. It is simply that in any company in which strategic planning is a principal tool of management rational decisions about social performance cannot be made and executed, with appropriate consideration for their cost and profit implications, outside the planning system. Divorcing social performance decisions from economic performance decisions deprives both of information essential for successful management in today's complex business environment.

77

The second problem is technical: developing a methodology for systematic description and prediction of evolving public attitudes—relating to business in general and to the specific company—parallel to and consistent with the treatment of economic, market, and technological conditions and trends. The critical issue here is not the acquisition of staff or outside consultant resources competent to provide projections and guidelines. These resources are available, although presently under-utilized. Much more important is the development in line and staff managers of an understanding of professional ideas, methods, and vocabulary so that managers who are responsible for planning can translate social forecasts into specific threats to and opportunities for a company's future business.

The same educational and experience deficiencies noted above with respect to the conceptual problem handicap line and staff managers. The motivation for encouraging them to address the problem is also identical. No amount of professional contribution can substitute for an operating manager's increased confidence and competence in converting social trends into facts of life for a profit-oriented business. The impressive record of corporate management in recent years in grasping economic and technological projections and applying them to strategy formulation and resource allocation should encourage an optimistic assessment of what managers can accomplish in handling social projections.

The third problem is procedural: management education and practice in detailed processes for incorporating social performance considerations in established business planning procedures. This calls for developing and using the skills and knowledge essential for describing and evaluating the costs, benefits, and risks associated with adopting, modifying, or rejecting specific social performance policies and· programs. The fundamental methodologies here are not significantly different from those involved in decisions on policies and programs related to economic performance. Nevertheless, they appear to be different to managers unaccustomed to treating them in a business context. Their strangeness can be removed only as members discover that familiar analytical procedures can be applied in formulating policy and resource decisions.

It may be reassuring to note that comparable procedural difficulties have been regularly met in introducing traditional long-range planning in organizations that have a history of operating within limited time horizons. The typical initial reaction among managers unaccustomed to extended planning horizons is that long-term trends have little relevance because they believe their business to be uniquely dependent on prompt responses to current and short-term conditions. Some believe that critical policy and resource decisions are largely intuitive and not susceptible to quantification and other structured evaluative techniques.

This familiar mixture of the "our business is different" and the "not invented here" syndromes can be overcome only by repeated demonstrations that planning horizons and measurement procedures are generally transferable across industry lines. As with all institutional change, acceptance of the planning process has been an experience of gradual accommodation, motivated by a growing recognition that it can work to produce a useful result. Extending the planning process to include social performance considerations will follow a similar pattern. An increasing number of companies are solving the procedural problems in exactly this way.

Projecting Long-Term Social Trends

Technical and procedural similarities between planning for economic performance and planning for social performance can be most easily identified by a description of the principal sequential steps in developing the strategic implications of social performance issues. In the course of doing this, specific differences will also emerge, as will the need for new knowledge, skills, and methods.

The first step is to identify the fundamental long-term forces that generate public dissatisfaction with specific aspects of existing business performance. Current demands for changes in business performance in such areas as environmental pollution, personnel practices, and consumer interests, for example, reflect underlying social trends the full effect of which probably is still to be determined. From comparable underlying economic forces emerge general economic expansion and contraction; growth, stabilization, and decay of product markets; inflationary thrusts in general and in specific costs and prices; cyclical and structural shifts in capital supply and demand; and other movements that constitute the familiar raw material of corporate planning for economic performance.

Underlying social forces exert similar tidal pressures on public attitudes and values. These, in turn, shape perceptions of benefits and injuries stemming from the practices of business organizations and the general business system. They also influence expectations for changes in business behavior that will minimize injuries, enhance existing benefits, or create new benefits. Unsatisfied expectations often lead to demands for legislation and regulation to reform business behavior.

These underlying social tides are as difficult to measure quantitatively as are underlying economic tides. Their general character and thrust are visible, however, and their general influences on the business environment can be described and evaluated. One of the most powerful of such forces in the United States and other industrialized democratic societies today is the erosion of the belief nurtured by the two-hundred-year flowering of the industrial and technological revolutions that economic growth will by its own momentum generate improvements in the quality of life enjoyed by all members of the society. Another is the mounting awareness of and sensitivity to disparities in benefits derived from economic expansion by groups within the society. A third is a spreading sense of the relative helplessness of the individual in an environment dominated by giant institutions, accompanied by a desire to assert and defend individual rights against institutional prerogatives.

Corporate managers need to understand how these underlying tidal forces influence social attitudes that are in turn sharpened and used by leaders of special interest constituencies. When managers grasp these relationships, even in the most general terms, they are intellectually ready to handle professionals' projections of specific social trends. They can then go on to translate these forecasts into pressures for changes in related aspects of business performance. As an analytical process this directly parallels the way in which managers translate relationships among underlying forces and developments in the general economy and in particular industries into specific opportunities for and threats to a single company.

No public concern with a social impact of business behavior has appeared suddenly and unheralded. Interest in quality of economic opportunity, protection of the environment against all types of contamination, safeguarding of consumer interests in market transactions and in product and service performance, and other manifestations of a broad desire for reform in the perceived behavior of business institutions have visible roots in underlying forces that have been developing for decades in American society.

Observers of social change have been studying and writing about these forces for many years. Expressions of mounting concern were flooding the news media in the 1950s and 1960s. It was, for example, repeatedly predicted in the 1950s that the pressure for removal of racial discrimination in access to public facilities in education, transportation, and other areas would inevitably extend to discriminatory personnel practices in public and private employment. It was expected that this thrust would broaden to include other forms of discrimination. It was repeatedly predicted by observers of social trends in the 1950s that the public's growing sensitivity to quality-of-life issues would develop into objections to air and water contamination and despoliation of natural resources. Consumerism in all its phases was visible and studied as an emerging trend in the 1950s, long before it organized the political power it now wields. Activist individuals and groups did not create these trends, although they surely gave forceful articulation to existing discontents and encouraged and assisted their social and political organization.

Most managers now recognize that all of these social developments have great significance. They impact on business policies and practices, and also on revenues, costs, and profits, with a force that approaches and sometimes equals that of economic, market, and technological developments. Corporate responses to these social developments have been generally reactive rather than anticipatory, tactical rather than strategic. The unfortunate result has been inadequate performance, far below the quality of responses to economic and technological developments. A number of companies have paid substantial penalties—in money and reputation—for these inadequacies. The business community as a whole has suffered a notable loss of public confidence and trust. The common complaint of business leaders that corporate behavior is now being judged by novel standards that were not applicable only a few years ago is itself evidence of their failure to be appropriately sensitive and responsive to social change.

The principal reason for this undesirable and unnecessary situation is the failure to incorporate social issues in the strategic planning process. Excluded from the planning process, almost every tactical social performance policy and program is viewed by managers as an impediment to the accomplishment of approved long-term goals and strategies. Since almost every corporate response to social pressure involves a decision to invest scarce resources that might otherwise be used to support profitable activities or a decision that adds to operating costs or complicates familiar administrative practices, it is not surprising that most managers at all levels view such responses as hostile to the traditional mission of business and, in personal terms, to the progress of their own careers. Social performance decisions that are not developed through the strategic planning process are rarely evaluated in relation to their accompanying social benefits. Nor are they assessed in the context of costly alternative constraints or penalties that might be mandated by society, or of constructive proposals for achieving desired results by more effective and efficient means.

Uncertainties in forecasting social trends—including their specific character, implications for business, probability of occurrence, and timing—should not deter their inclusion in the formal strategic planning process. Executives surely need no reminder about similar uncertainties in economic projections. They are aware of the improvements in economic forecasting that have resulted from several decades of professional study of the causes of economic growth, stagnation, and decline. They know how experience in relating general economic projections to prospects for specific industries and companies has contributed to more effective planning.

Against this background, it is reasonable to anticipate that comparable professional and managerial appraisal of the trust and meaning of social trends will over time improve the quality of forecasting in this area. In any event, what is immediately important is not precision in describing social trends and interpreting their meaning for future public expectations and demands for changes in business behavior. Rather, it is explicit recognition in the planning process that these trends are significant and should be considered in resource allocation decisions and in formulating related corporate policies and programs.

Translating Social Trends into Claims on Business Behavior

The second step in integrating social performance within the corporate strategic planning system is to identify the specific claims on business policies and practices that are likely to evolve from broad social trends. The conceptual parallel between economic and social forecasting reappears here. Free-floating futurism in either the economic or the social realm is an engaging intellectual game. It begins to capture management attention only when projections of underlying tidal movements are translated into specific business opportunities and threats, which in turn provide a basis for planning, including appropriate offensive and defensive strategies and supporting action programs.

Some familiar recent developments provide convenient illustrations. Only a few years ago mounting concern about the damaging side effects of economic growth translated into a "quality-of-life" movement that rapidly identified areas of interest to a variety of constituencies. Activist groups took the lead in publicizing claims of specific damage to the society as a result of widespread business practices. It soon became apparent that many of the claims were enlisting rather broad public support. The general situation at this stage roughly resembled that in the economic area when many people were becoming sensitive to the implications of sustained inflation and were revising established saving and spending patterns.

In the social area, public sensitivity to quality-of-life issues could have been translated by perceptive observers into specific pressures for reform of business practices in polluting or otherwise injuring the environment. A reasonable reading of this development by alert business planners would have provided early warning of both opportunities and threats to entire industries (chemicals, paper, steel, coal mining, to name a few), as well as to individual companies or divisions of companies in these and other industries. The sighted opportunities and threats would then have served as significant inputs for corporate planning. Depending on particular circumstances, including evaluations of economic and social costs and benefits, individual companies might have blueprinted rational offensive and defensive strategies and action programs. One planning option clearly would have been to organize single-company, industry-wide, and other initiatives at federal, state, and local levels to influence both positively and negatively the shaping of the predictable remedial legislation.

Another illustration is provided by the conjunction after World War II of multiple movements favoring greater social, political, and economic equality. The power inherent in this thrust was generated by its combination of those who were victimized by discrimination which they were determined to end, those who were morally repelled by discrimination practiced against others, and those who on practical grounds feared that continued discrimination would wound American society and invite disturbances that would threaten personal security and property rights. As important social institutions, corporations could not avoid either responsibility for discriminatory personnel practices within their organizations or the effects of remedial actions that would be stimulated by the groups determined for various reasons to remove gross inequalities from our society.

From the viewpoint of business planners, this tidal thrust toward equality was as likely to affect business policies and behavior as, we can now observe, was the organization of an international petroleum producers' cartel and the subsequent decision to quadruple the world price of oil. Further, sophisticated observers of social trends were predicting that the initial focus on equal access for blacks to public services and facilities would rapidly extend to jobs and careers and would expand to include every other population segment that was in any way disadvantaged—socially, economically, politically, legally. In effect, encapsulated in the original black protest were claims for across-the-board equality of treatment for Hispanics, Indians, women, old people, young people, other racial and ethnic groups, religious groups, homosexuals. Even more important, like the blacks, all would be demanding correction of and compensation for prior inequities. Their later appearance making explicit organized demands for equal rights was as predictable after the initial black protests of the late 1940s and early 1950s as were the worldwide economic repercussions of OPEC's price manipulation.

An early evaluation of the equal-rights movement by perceptive corporate planners would have identified significant opportunities and threats for business institutions in general and for individual companies. On the opportunity side was the possibility for timely initiatives to get rid of discriminatory practices in a manner and on a schedule that would minimize internal strains of adjustment. Farseeing corporate leadership could have placed itself in a position of substantial compliance with the legislation that was surely coming. In so doing, it could have protected itself from the embarrassment and cost of complying under a mandate and on a schedule that permitted inadequate time for adjustment and accommodation. Beyond this, companies moving early to erase discrimination in hiring and career progress would have benefited from the chance to employ and promote the most talented people in previously untapped reservoirs of human resources. On the defensive or threat side, alert managements could have initiated exploration of such particularly sensitive and difficult areas as seniority rights, job assignments, middle- and junior-management understanding of changing personnel policies and competence to apply them, supervisory skills in working with minority employees, and adequacy of indoctrination and training programs.

The development during the past two decades of a powerful movement to protect consumer interests is another example of the transformation of a broadly based general concern into specific claims on business. No one sensitive to social ground swells could have failed to observe the appearance of local consumer groups or to speculate that a charismatic activist might move onto the national stage to articulate their discontents. That activist happened to be Ralph Nader. If he had not seized the assignment, however, another individual would surely have exploited the opportunity. Corporate planners with a charter encompassing more than economic and technological trends would have had occasion for timely assessment of the implications of organized consumerism with its inherent opportunities and threats, and for the formulation of appropriate offensive and defensive strategies.

The value of such early recognition and perceptive planning, particularly by corporations with a major stake in consumer confidence and goodwill, is beyond debate. The market behavior of a few companies suggests this kind of sensitivity and programmed response. Lethargic performance by most consumer-oriented companies must bear principal responsibility for much of the widespread distrust and criticism of business behavior and for the flood of protective legislation, most of it designed by uninformed enthusiasts with little regard for normal technological, production, and marketing practices.

It may be useful to note several current social and socioeconomic developments, which, while still at an early stage, should be under observation and evaluation by business planners. One is the growing conflict between multinational economic organizations and mononational political organizations. The discontinuities between these inherently incompatible power structures parallel on the world scene the troubled relationships within the U.S. between business engaged in interstate commerce and state regulatory jurisdictions. Here the attempted resolution has been the creation of a complex of national regulatory bodies with a mixed record of accomplishment and a jungle of continuing jurisdictional confusions in the areas of control standards and taxation. It offers one, but not the only, possible model for the world situation. Multinational business in general and individual corporations in particular have a clear planning interest in the problem, including the opportunity to initiate constructive proposals in competition with the impractical and even destructive ideas that already are being promoted by supporters of statism at the country, regional, or world level.

A second development with potential significance for corporate planning at the social interface is the appearance of efforts to introduce constitutional bill-of-rights and due-process concepts into personnel administration. Sensitive issues here include standards and procedures in assignment, promotion, and discharge decisions; protection of internal "free speech" and "whistle-blowing"; and grievance policies and practices beyond those prescribed in union contracts. These issues suggest questions bearing on the design of long-range plans for employee relations, with the usual array of offensive and defensive strategic options.

A third development is the initial voicing of an interest in arrangements for guaranteed working-lifetime employment. Whether in the manner usually associated with the Japanese industrial practice or in other ways, there is increasing evidence, on both labor and management sides, of curiosity about the possible benefits and costs that might be involved in various types of guarantees of continuous employment. Even superficial evaluation suggests that the net balance of positive and negative considerations is likely to be strongly affected by the unique economic and market circumstances of the individual firm, as well as the values of its senior management and the internal environment created by its experience of employee relations. Regardless of the intuitive hostility of many corporate executives to the notion of institutionalizing cost rigidities—a legitimate and substantial concern—the possibility of swelling popular support for greater worker income security is in itself sufficient reason for using the planning process to identify and assess specific costs, benefits, and risks associated with the options realistically available to a company.

A fourth development is the public discussion of relationships between job content and work process, on one side, and the level of employee morale and productivity on the other. There is an increasing flow of descriptive reporting of experiments here and abroad in "job enrichment" and employee participation in designing the work process and in related decisions generally regarded as managerial in nature. There is also a growing body of theory, or at least efforts to formulate and test theory, bearing on the influence of job content and method on human behavior in fulfilling task assignments. The generally mediocre record of employee productivity and commitment to organizational goals, about which so many managers complain, underlies the importance of enlarging the corporate planning process to include evaluation of ways and means to improve long-range profitability by fresh approaches to the roles and duties of workers.

From Social Trends to Specific Business Strategies

The third step in integrating social performance considerations within the strategic planning system is to identify feasible policies and programs that are responsive to important societal needs and claims. This requires an evaluation of the benefits and costs of all options available to the company, including the option of doing nothing. Such an evaluation will include judgments about relative priorities and timing among socially responsive strategic options, as well as cross-relationships among social and economic programs and policies. It is not simple to make this probing evaluation, of course. But neither is it impossible. In fact, comparable evaluations are made regularly in the normal planning process with respect to economic, market, and technological issues.

Two principal criteria should be applied in assessing social trends as a basis for formulating specific business strategies. The first criterion is the relative importance to a company, through its normal planning period, of identified social trends. The second is the feasibility of developing and executing relevant strategies. Both criteria can be applied through systematic analyses that follow familiar evaluation procedures in corporate economic, market, and technological planning. In this context, as all managers know, a decision to do nothing is a legitimate strategic decision as important for planning purposes as a commitment to a positive course of action, and equally freighted with potential for good or bad results.

For the individual corporation, the relative importance of perceived social trends is directly determined by the unique characteristics of its business. For labor-intensive companies, the full range of pressures for equitable personnel practices is of top urgency, including demands for correction of past inequities. For manufacturers and marketers of consumer products, as well as for providers of consumer services, a high priority must be assigned to claims for protection of consumer interests of all types, in the areas of advertising techniques and claims, financing methods and terms, product performance and safety, and service and other guarantees. For companies whose extraction or processing activities degrade the environment, there can be no doubt about the critical planning issue. Multiproduct companies, particularly those involved in a variety of industries and production technologies, face planning urgencies that are determined by unique divisional characteristics.

For any corporation at a particular time in its ongoing operating experience, a judgment on relative importance should be qualified by an accompanying judgment on relative urgency. The "first things first" doctrine is as relevant in analyzing optional responses to societal claims as in weighing available strategic moves in response to economic, market, and technological developments. Assessments of urgency may be influenced by the momentum and power of trends and forces in the external environment and also those acting within the organization. In common experience, these factors are often interactive and thereby magnified in urgency.

The second criterion above—feasibility of developing and executing effective responsive strategies—is likely to be a more restrictive screening test. Economic, legal, and organizational considerations require evaluation. In some circumstances, political considerations related to competitors' attitudes and market power may also be important.

The economic costs directly associated with many types of corporate social performance need to be evaluated with respect to their impact on revenues and expenses. It is not in the interest of responsible corporate managers or of the investors whose property they administer to take any action likely adversely to affect competitive economic performance or prospects. Nor is it reasonable for outsiders concerned with bringing about specific changes in corporate behavior to expect voluntary initiatives by individual companies in such circumstances, when the economic judgments are well documented.

Economic costs can become a trap for superficial appraisal, however. It is always easy and often tempting for managers to view incremental expenses related to improved social performance as burdens without compensating benefits. In specific situations, these additional costs may generate both economic and social returns. It is essential to probe for the possible existence of such compensating balances and to evaluate the extent to which their contribution may offset associated expenses. Investment in pollution control may on occasion yield commercially marketable by-products in addition to community environment benefits. Direct and indirect costs associated with more equitable personnel policies and practices may be accompanied in specific circumstances by economic and social gains within the organization, in addition to external social benefits. Costs involved in responding to pressures for protection of consumer interests may help to create profitable and competitively advantageous marketing opportunities. Investments aimed at upgrading the safety and hygiene of working conditions are often associated with a variety of positive returns in employee retention, productivity, and insurance charges, over and above the obvious personnel benefits.

All relevant economic and social gains should be identified and evaluated in relation to applicable costs before reaching a conclusion on the net effect of any proposed investment in improved social performance. The widespread public skepticism, so often documented in opinion surveys, about business claims that upgrading social performance is uneconomic in general terms and competitively disadvantageous in specific situations reflects a public perception that business institutions are insufficiently responsive to societal claims. Imaginative business leadership should recognize the positive aspects of social investment and be prepared to document negative judgments in specific circumstances.

Consideration of costs associated with not responding to pressures for improved social performance should be an integral part of the evaluation of costs and benefits. Unfavorable publicity, damaged corporate reputation, legal expenses, fines and other regulatory and judicial penalties, and weakened market position are all costs to be appraised on the way to the ultimate judgment that a particular responsive social strategy is or is not practical and feasible.

The central issue is simply that the corporate planning process for social performance commitments should be comprehensive in scope. So far as possible, it should be free from intuitive bias against the introduction of social performance considerations in coordination with economic performance considerations. In short, it should be guided by operational rather than philosophical considerations.

Organizational matters that require assessment in planning for social performance are related to two familiar conditions in companies in which middle-level executives are responsible for formulating operating unit plans to be evaluated higher in the organization structure. One is the natural disposition of middle managers to focus planning attention on those dimensions of their jobs that their experience identifies as prime sources of career pay-offs. The other is their disposition to concentrate on activities over which they perceive themselves able to exercise a reasonable measure of control.

The meaning of these conditions is clear. Plans moving upstream for senior-management review are not likely to incorporate significant and realistic social performance content unless the middle managers who prepare the plans know they are responsible for both economic and social performance and know that their career progress will be determined by their record of appropriately balanced accomplishment in both areas. They will develop this knowledge through sustained and consistent exposure to three interrelated influences. One is educational: understanding senior management's assessment of the forces moving in our society for modifying the traditional role and responsibility of business institutions and for their consequent behavior. A second is policy and procedure guidance: explicit identification of organizational goals redefined to include social performance objectives in coordination with economic performance objectives, reinforced by specific planning guidelines and procedures that demonstrate how these related objectives are to be handled in the planning process. And the third is operational: visible provision for measuring and rewarding middle managers' implementation of the social commitments in approved plans in a manner that parallels the attention paid to implementation of economic commitments.

Failure to apply all three influences concurrently will substantially weaken middle managers' belief in the integrity of the organization's announced commitment to social performance objectives, as well as their understanding of the specific terms through which a balanced accommodation of economic and social considerations is to be secured. In combination, of course, the influences amount to a redesign of the planning system to reflect a broad corporate policy commitment and to assure a solid bridge between policy and operations.

5

Measuring Corporate Social Performance

Rational administration of corporate social performance requires systematic information about resource
inputs and result outputs in terms that facilitate managerial judgments about costs, priorities, effectiveness,
efficiency, and return on investment. Creating such an
information system is complicated by the fact that some
of the social performance inputs and many of the outputs
are beyond the range of traditional business activities.
Established financial, accounting, and operating information systems were not designed to meet social performance needs for decision and control information. Most
of the relevant information simply does not exist in organized form. Even more significant, for all but a few
companies some of the fundamental issues involved in
designing the underlying information system are yet to be
identified and their implications assessed in relation to
specific needs for decision and control.

This deficiency is not wholly negative. It may, indeed,

be advantageous. Significant progress toward social performance objectives need not await the supply of the missing information. As managers begin to think about social performance concepts and how to mesh them with economic performance objectives, they will develop valuable ideas about the general character and detailed composition of a desirable information base. The work involved in providing that base can then proceed concurrently with a company's growing involvement with social performance policies and programs. Such a coordinated growth of information requirements and supply will help to discourage ill-considered efforts to generate information that may turn out to have minimum operating utility. It will also inhibit the familiar tendency to design costly new information systems in advance of demonstrated managerial needs.

Those who argue that new information systems must provide precise quantitative measures of social performance inputs and outputs have a naive view of business operations. They ignore the fact that beneath the surface appearance of precision and accuracy presented by traditional financial and cost accounting data lie gross approximations whose operational utility ordinarily is not materially impaired by their imprecision. They ignore the common observation of sophisticated managers that decision making may be as much confused and delayed by excessive and irrelevant information as it is assisted by hard data that illuminate critical issues in resource allocation and performance evaluation. They also ignore the fact that quality of management judgment often contributes more to successful performance than quantity of specific data.

The sound way to proceed is to let emerging operational requirements determine the general character and specific content of the information base, and to build that base step by step to service the organization's expanding social performance activities. This will produce a diversified inventory of social performance information, with elements varying in nature, quality, and detail. Some information can be drawn or adapted from the existing financial and cost accounting system. Other information needs will require new sources, such as special surveys within the company or data available from supplier, industry, or government sources. Some information, particularly on the input side, will be expressed in rather precise quantitative terms. Other information may be available only in qualitative terms. At a later time, when a company's total social performance program has been clearly defined, when its management experience with social performance is substantial, and when its needs for decision and control information have been subjected to the test of operational applications, there will be opportunities for systematic coordination of all social performance information and even for consolidating much social performance information within a comprehensive financial accounting system. This kind of piecemeal growth, eventually leading to considerable (but probably not total) integration, is precisely the evolutionary path followed over decades in the financial and cost accounting area. It should serve as a model for developing information for social performance activities.

Techniques for Generating Information

Three principal techniques can be used in generating information for managing corporate social performance. The first is descriptive—qualitative rather than quantitative in concept. The second uses cost-benefit comparisons adapted from analytical methods initially developed to facilitate military resource planning decisions. The third applies standard financial accounting methodology.

The three approaches can fairly be viewed as complementary rather than mutually exclusive. They represent an ascending scale of sophistication and precision in management information. An organization that begins with qualitative description will soon discover opportunities for quantification of some of the information required for decision and control. Simple quantification provides a foundation for comparing at least some costs and related benefits. The use of cost-benefit concepts tends to stimulate creative ideas for broadening and deepening the application of the technique. As this occurs, possibilities are likely to be identified for applying or adapting standard financial accounting methods to social performance information needs. While the ultimate goal of full integration of social performance measurements within a single comprehensive corporate financial accounting system may be unattainable, and is certainly remote, its presence on the horizon cannot fail to be a constructive influence for continual improvement in the volume and detail of social performance information.

The Descriptive Audit

Two considerations should motivate senior corporate officers to undertake at least a verbal description of social performance resource inputs and results. The first is external pressures, ranging from hostile assessments of business activities portrayed as socially harmful to neutral or friendly curiosity about the range and effects of activities seen as possibly or certainly socially beneficial. The other consideration is internal, reflecting an essential first step by management that is sensitive to changing public expectations for business behavior and therefore is concerned to identify socially positive and negative activities as a basis for determining both contributions and vulnerabilities. The somewhat ambitious phrase "social performance audit" has been applied to a structured description of a company's socially related activities.

In its simplest form the audit may be no more than verbal description, possibly reinforced by a few numbers where data are readily available. On the positive side, a typical audit might describe a company's programs to assure equitable employment and career opportunities for minorities and women; its contributions to philanthropic, educational, and artistic organizations; its investments to reduce environmental pollution and increase internal safety and hygiene; its support of employee education and training; its various forms of responses to community problems and needs; and its policies and practices designed to protect consumer interests in product purchase and use. On the negative side, the audit might describe inadequacies, relative to government, community, or internal company standards, in any of these areas.

A descriptive audit of this character—comparable to those prepared by a small but growing group of companies in recent years—can serve a number of valuable purposes. First and most important, it makes available to top management (including outside directors) a comprehensive status report that portrays the full potential range of social performance concern and identifies areas of strength and weakness in a way that cannot fail to be both informative and educational. Such a statement may reveal laggard execution of corporate policy (for example, in implementing an announced commitment to nondiscriminatory personnel administration), insensitivity to community pressures in the areas of pollution or social services, or failure to take advantage of opportunities to strengthen market position by perceptive adaptation of product and service offerings to changing consumer concerns. On the positive side, the audit may turn up instances of favorable social performance not previously viewed in this light by senior management because the actions were taken for reasons not directly related to their social impact.

On both positive and negative fronts, such a report is likely to enhance management's perception of the growing significance of social performance issues and management's sensitivity to specific areas of opportunity and vulnerability. It may also contribute to the development of a common understanding among senior executives of the broad policy implications of a corporate commitment to coordinate social and economic performance objectives.

Several related purposes will be served by the initial audit. It is likely to provide material that can be reported in favorable terms to a variety of publics, including shareholders, employees, special interest groups, plant communities, and, where appropriate, customers. It begins the process of alerting middle managers to top management's concern about the social implications of operating policies and practices. This will prepare the way for any future changes that may be instituted in areas in which their support will be required for effective action. It will illuminate inconsistent practices among operating units. The experience of making the audit will highlight deficiencies and gaps in relevant information and will suggest opportunities for introducing quantitative measures to provide more solid documentation. Finally, if the audit process is institutionalized, as in an announced commitment to repeat it annually, it can become an instrument for motivating efforts to improve performance even when such progress can be described only in qualitative terms.

Three points should be clearly understood about such a descriptive or qualitative audit. The first is that the audit is not a planning tool. While contributing in a rudimentary way to identifying issues that should be incorporated in the planning process, it yields no information on two subjects that require careful exploration before they can be handled realistically in planning. One of these subjects is the resource requirements to implement social performance policies and programs, together with assessments of probable direct results and positive and negative side effects. The other is the status and likely future of societal expectations and demands for changed behavior by business in general, by the industry of which a specific company is a part, and by the company itself. Systematic assessments of both subjects will call for information far beyond the scope of a descriptive audit, which simply undertakes to identify the company's posture in areas of current and potential social concern.

The second point is that the descriptive audit does not evaluate in any way what a company has done or has failed to do in areas of social concern. Evaluation requires criteria or standards with which performance can be compared. The two relevant sources of performance standards are, of course, the external society and internal top management. Standards emanating from both sources will exert a critical influence on the determination of social performance objectives through the long-range planning process, and on the policies and programs that are developed to accomplish those goals. It would not be advantageous, however, to introduce, directly or by implication, the concept of evaluative criteria in the initial phase of the descriptive audit. On the contrary, it should be made clear to all participating managers that the purpose is simply to ascertain in a systematic way what the organization is doing and where it stands.

The third point is that the results of the descriptive audit are strictly for internal management use. After reviewing the audit's findings, management may conclude that certain information generated through the audit process should be communicated in appropriate form to selected publics. Such a possible use should not be a consideration in the decision to undertake the audit, however. Anticipation of this use might in one way or another contaminate the internal reporting environment and skew some managers' responses toward an unduly favorable portrayal of status and practices.

Within these constraints, the chief executive officer will find the descriptive audit an instrument with informational, educational, and motivational values in the initial phase of determining his company's social performance posture and preparing for the more probing analysis that must precede decisions for or against a more ambitious effort. While the administrative burden of organizing and implementing a first-time descriptive audit is not negligible, it is modest in relation to the benefits likely to be realized. To assure these benefits, however, an effort must be made to achieve both comprehensive coverage of socially significant activity areas and comparability of reporting among operating units. Neither of these objectives should be treated casually.

In a large organization engaged in producing and marketing a diversified product line at multiple locations it will be particularly important not to overload the system with an initial information request that is cumbersome in bulk and complex in detail. At least three good reasons counsel moderation in approaching operating management. First, the problems of providing social performance information about such varied installations and activities cannot be fully anticipated at the outset. Unforeseen reporting difficulties and misunderstandings are likely to surface, and their appearance as impediments to adequate response by operating units will sap operating managers' confidence in the exercise. Second, an information request that strikes operating managers as unreasonably onerous is an invitation to resistance, delay, and superficial treatment. Third, even if all information sought in a survey that appears massive in length and depth should be provided, top management would not know how to use it.

The governing rationale for such an information request can only be that it will yield essential data support for specific social performance decision and control purposes. These specific purposes will become clear to top management at a considerably later stage and cannot be anticipated with any confidence by executives who are only beginning to think about corporate social performance as a significant factor in charting a long-term course for a business. Since the immediate objective is limited to a general picture of a company's social performance position, the initial survey should be appropriately simple in form. It should invite descriptive responses supported by quantitative information only where such data are readily available. It should instruct responding managers to supplement their answers to survey questions with informal observations on actions, or absence of actions, in areas they judge to be socially sensitive in the context of their own operations and community environments.

The responses to such a broad-brush initial survey will serve a number of useful purposes. Operating managers who have been encouraged to apply independent judgment to what they report will reveal a good deal about the state of their perceptions of issues and problems at the business-society interface. This is important information for senior executives because the attitudes and values relating to corporate social performance that prevail down through the organization hierarchy are critical considerations in deciding how to implement whatever policies and practices top management ultimately adopts. The responses will illuminate differences among organizational units in existing social performance conditions and activities. In one division, for example, local management may be committed to, and well along in executing, nondiscriminatory personnel career practices, while other units have been slow to place minorities and women in supervisory positions because of management hostility, indifference, or concentration on other administrative problems. The responses will indicate significant differences among areas of perceived concern to plant communities or interest groups, reflecting local environmental or labor market conditions. Finally, the responses will illuminate the need for a more structured second-stage survey, ways to design such an inquiry, and opportunities to substitute quantitative for qualitative descriptions of social peformance status and actions.

In short, the principal contribution of an initial free-form and open-ended survey of the kind here suggested is in building a base for a more thorough descriptive audit. In this second stage, the information sought can be defined with considerable precision. If, for example, one information objective is to determine the extent to which minorities and women hold management positions, the questionnaire can request for each defined management tier the total number of positions, number of positions filled by blacks, by women, etc. If another information objective is to determine the extent and nature of local management involvement in community affairs and assistance in ameliorating community problems, responses in this area in the initial survey will facilitate calling for specific identification of contributions to philanthropic, educational, artistic, and other institutions; managers' support of local organizations; employees' participation in staffing or otherwise assisting special education programs for youths or adults; investments in reducing or removing specific causes of air or water pollution; etc.

The target for the second-stage survey remains, as in the initial survey, a description of social performance status and activities. However, the more structured character of the survey should make it possible to prescribe the specific areas for which information is requested, define the precise terms in which information is to be reported, and request quantitative responses for some information categories and a specific pattern of qualitative responses for other areas. As a result, the responses will be susceptible to aggregation—partly in quantitative terms, partly in verbal terms—and the end product will be a valid general description of the organization's social performance status and activities.

Getting this far should not be viewed as only an information-collecting exercise of limited operational utility. Beyond the informational, educational, and motivational benefits noted above, the descriptive audit serves as a transition mechanism to several operational strategies. First and probably most obvious, in such sensitive areas as personnel administration and direction of procurement to minority-owned supplier firms, information generated through the audit process can be used as a base line for measuring future progress. Specific goals can be identified and their accomplishment evaluated. Second, the organization's position in other sensitive areas such as environmental pollution and plant safety and hygiene can be evaluated in relation to three significant criteria: applicable legal requirements, industry practices formally reported or informally known to management, and management's internal standards as determined by its values and priorities. Third, audit information may suggest areas where judgments about the feasibility and desirability of responding to perceived or anticipated external pressures for changed social performance clearly depend on much more thorough analysis of costs and results. Here the audit's function is to alert top management to the need for targeting research on resource requirements, benefits, side effects, and the complex interactions between economic and social performance. Some types of environmental and plant situations raise problems of this character. So, too, do questions of product safety and other issues within the scope of what is loosely viewed as "consumerism."

Beyond these applications—and the examples are meant to be suggestive, not inclusive—the audit will indicate the socially sensitive areas in which operating divisions have been wholly or relatively inactive. Here top management has an opportunity to appraise the economic, political, and organizational implications of permitting the status quo to continue, as well as an opportunity to evaluate costs and benefits associated with positive initiatives.

Cost-Benefit Analysis

A familiar criticism of proposals to incorporate social performance considerations within overall business planning and policy formulation argues that some of the costs and many of the benefits associated with social performance cannot be measured in quantitative terms. Critics point out that social performance inputs and outputs are fundamentally different from those processed through the expense-revenue calculations of standard financial accounting. How does a company measure in meaningful terms, they ask, the costs to itself and to society of inequitable personnel practices, or the costs and benefits associated with doing away with such practices? How does it measure the social costs of its continuing pollution of society's air or water? The costs of reducing or eliminating pollution are probably determinable, but how assess the social benefits of diminished pollution? Those who are skeptical about the possibility of managing corporate social performance in the context of maximizing a firm's long-term profitability are fond of extending these conundrums to almost every aspect of business behavior that is the target of social criticism.

These are not trivial issues. The questions are appropriate, and they are directed at substantive problems. In developing answers to the questions—and it should be noted that there are practical answers—two points need to be held clearly in mind. The first is that corporate social performance is not the first resource allocation decision area in which these types of problems have appeared. Many corporations have had limited experience and some governmental organizations, notably the Department of Defense, have had extensive experience with analyzing cost and benefits in situations where some of the decision elements are not fully measured by financial accounting methodology. This experience is directly relevant in handling many of the decision problems encountered in the social performance area.

The second point is that business managers make decisions every day in circumstances where at least part of the information input provides measures of "more" or "less" without specifying "how much." The language of numbers and the grammar of arithmetic create a superficial appearance of precision. In fact, as experienced managers know, in most major resource decision situations the critical determining factor is judgment, not precision of information. The quality of judgment is partially derived from the quantity and quality of the available relevant information, to be sure. But information alone, no matter how comprehensive, detailed, and seemingly precise it may be, is not allowed to "make" decisions whose outcome can have a substantial effect on operating results. The absence of apparent precision of information in many social performance decision situations is a significant but not a controlling consideration.

The primary reason for the limited applicability of currently available financial accounting information to the measurement of corporate social performance is that financial accounting has been developed for the principal purpose of measuring relationships between monetary revenues and monetary costs. Indeed, its dedication to this purpose explains the growth of supplemental measuring systems designed to serve additional management information needs of measurement and control of production, marketing, and other business activities. Since resource allocation decisions related to social performance also involve considerations—some on the cost side, many on the benefit side—beyond those normally handled in existing financial accounting methodology, supplemental information is required. On the cost side, relevant information often includes measures of what economists call opportunity costs—opportunities or benefits forgone when a specific course of action is selected from several available alternatives. On the benefit side, relevant information often includes measures of the nonfinancial results of social performance programs within the firm and in its external environment.

The methodology known variously as cost-benefit, cost-effectiveness, or, most broadly, systems analysis has been applied to handle this type of problem in some aspects of strategic planning in business and more extensively in governmental strategic planning in the military and some other public sectors. The methodology is designed to aid, but not replace, the judgments of decision makers; to improve the quality of those judgments by more precise, systematic statement of problems and alternatives and by facilitating comparisons among alternatives; and to combine the maximum feasible quantification with related structured qualitative measurements.

In its application to managing corporate social performance, the methodology goes beyond the descriptive audit. The descriptive audit identifies existing conditions and ongoing policies and programs. It can also serve to establish base lines for further progress. It does not assist decision making, however, except by its identification of areas where decisions may be required or desirable. Cost-benefit analysis can supplement the audit by organizing and facilitating the decision process, and in addition, when applied repetitively it can contribute to measurement and control. It is particularly useful in dealing with comparisons of the "better than" and "worse than" kind as against the absolute concept inherent in "maximizing." Lest this be viewed as heresy, it should be promptly noted that, contrary to popular mythology, the real aim of business managers is not profit maximization, since it is impossible to define maximum attainable profitability. The practical objective must be expressed in some sense of "better than"— better than last year, better than the competition, better than some objective benchmark.

Examples of applications of cost-benefit analysis suggest its potential contribution to effective management of corporate social performance. In private industry, the cost-benefit technique is used (although not always so identified) when management assesses the relative advantages of making, or not making, each of several optional investments in product design in circumstances in which the alternative costs are quantitatively determined while the alternative results (benefits) are estimated in terms of effects on sales, price, market share, and other relevant variables. In the Department of Defense, the cost-benefit technique is used in selecting an advantageous mix of offensive instrumentalities (piloted bombers, land-based missiles, sea-based missiles, satellite-based missiles) and defensive instrumentalities (piloted interceptor aircraft, land-based antimissile missiles, civil defense measures). In the nondefense public sector, the technique is used in analyzing costs and benefits of alternative water resource projects, alternative health programs, alternative urban transportation programs, and other areas.

The cost-benefit methodology can be advantageously applied to a variety of social performance decision and control situations, provided that management understands that the purpose is to contribute to better-informed and therefore more effective decision making, but nothing so ambitious as maximization. The following examples will suggest some of the possibilities of going beyond simple description of social performance status and process to systematic cost-benefit analysis that combines feasible quantification with qualitative comparative evaluation.

Almost all large and most medium-sized corporations now make annual appropriations for philanthropic, educational, artistic, and other nonprofit purposes. Informal surveys indicate that only a few firms attempt a systematic analysis of costs and related external and internal benefits with a view to improving the social performance effectiveness of their donations. In most organizations the common procedure is that top management determines the gross annual donation budget, within which allocations are made to applicant organizations by a management committee. The gross budget is usually set at a percentage of total revenues, consistent with that approved in recent years. The typical schedule of grants in an individual company reflects some combination of the established pattern of annual gifts, specific recommendations of a few senior executives (often influenced by "arm-twisting" solicitations from business or personal friends), and periodic community pressures to contribute to special one-time causes such as an urban renewal project, a local recreation facility, or a new or enlarged community hospital. Seldom is as much as an informal effort made to analyze even in descriptive terms the relation of real costs to real benefits associated with approved and rejected grant applications, with the objective of improving the estimated benefit-cost ratio.

Cost-benefit analysis can be advantageously applied in evaluating potential investment in pollution reduction or elimination. Capital and operating costs associated with a specific project are, of course, quantitatively determinable. So, too, are costs and revenues associated with possible commercial use of by-products of pollution control. When available, tax and other economic benefits can be calculated. But the purpose of diminishing environmental contamination is to reduce social costs and increase social benefits. Foul air has a direct impact on the health and life expectancy of those exposed to it. It also affects some household maintenance and laundry and drycleaning costs. Foul rivers and lakes and seashores exert similar negative influences, and also curtail opportunities for recreation and related quality-of-life considerations. The presence of both types of pollution can be significant constraints on a community's ability to attract new job-

creating, tax-paying business, and on the ability of existing business to recruit and retain managerial and professional talent. The degree of environmental beneficiation
associated with specific pollution control projects can be
specifically determined, and at least gross qualitative
judgments can be made about the related social benefits.

These determinations and judgments are worth making as significant elements in a comprehensive evaluation of the options confronting a senior-management
group that is sensitive to broadly held community attitudes toward business behavior and to the implications
of continuing a "business as usual" posture. The outcome
of such an evaluation might well be different for a company that is the major polluter in a community than for a
company that is a minor contributor to environmental
contamination. It would certainly be different in a situation in which the net economic cost of an antipollution
project and the anticipated effect on competitive position
are of modest magnitude than it would be where the net
cost and competitive impacts are substantial. Consideration of social costs and benefits together with immediate
and longer-term economic costs in a single decision calculus is not designed, it should be remembered, to assure
a different investment decision. Rather, the objective is
to provide a broader information base for a better investment decision in the context of a society that is modifying the values that bear on business decisions. It was
precisely these considerations in an encompassing cost-
benefit assessment that influenced the business leadership of Pittsburgh after World War II to undertake a
common commitment to clean up that city's air and
water environment.

The analytical logic of cost-benefit analysis can be
applied in a variety of other business actions that impact
a variety of "publics." Improvement of safety and

hygiene of the work place involves quantitatively determinable increases in overhead costs of facilities, which can be allocated in familiar ways to units of output. The investment is also likely, on the benefit side, to enhance employees' morale and productivity, reduce personnel turnover and recruitment and training costs, and, for some industries, diminish long-term health hazards and the associated risks of damage suits and unfavorable publicity. These effects are measurable in a combination of quantitative and qualitative terms. Unequal personnel practices that discriminate against minorities and women represent quantitatively indeterminate but describable social costs that can be compared with the net balance of short-term economic benefits in the form of lower labor costs (as against those of "equal pay for equal work") and longer-term economic costs resulting from higher turnover of dissatisfied victims of inequitable pay and promotion practices, as well as possible legal costs, loss of government contracts, and unfavorable publicity.

Consideration of the large number of current business practices that generate costs for the external society and of existing and potential improvements in corporate social performance that produce social benefits suggests the practical value of systematically balancing economic and social costs against economic and social benefits. The presence of indeterminate elements on one side or the other of these comparisons creates a certain degree of fuzziness, to be sure. But this is no greater proportion of uncertainty than experienced managers regularly handle in critical resource decision situations in which pay-offs on investments in R & D, political developments, or the hazards of the judicial process are significant variables. Viewed in this context, cost-benefit concepts can be a valuable tool for measurement and control in managing corporate social performance.

Financial Accounting

That there are complex conceptual and practical problems in applying the science and art of traditional financial accounting to measuring corporate social performance is beyond debate. On the conceptual side, one source of difficulty is confusion about the purpose of social performance measurement. Is the main objective of measurement to facilitate reporting to shareholders, communities, and other external publics in meaningful terms? Or is it to facilitate managerial decision making and control? The distinction is significant because choice between the alternatives can lead to quite different quantitative measurement systems. One of these (management-oriented) could be reasonably consistent with financial accounting methodology, while the other (public-relations-oriented) might, and for maximum effectiveness probably should, take a different structure and terminology. Reconciliation between the two systems would require gross judgmental accommodations.

The argument of this book favors the primacy of management's need for information to improve both the quality of resource decisions relating to social performance and the effectiveness of administrative control of the implementation of these decisions. The use of information for external reporting of actions and results is of secondary, although certainly not negligible, importance. Acceptance of this priority should simplify thinking about applying accounting systems to social performance. It will not, to be sure, resolve all problems. But the application of accounting techniques to economic performance is still, after several hundred years, not quite trouble-free.

A second difficulty arises in handling social performance policies and programs that have no readily identified substantial direct costs yet provide important ben-

115

efits to external publics and often to the sponsoring company as well. Improvements in product safety and performance—by no means always brought about with negligible costs, of course—may provide examples of this situation. So, too, may abatement of uninformative or misleading advertising practices, or, for food products, increased nutritional value. Nondiscriminatory personnel practices may be enforced with little direct expense— although in some circumstances there are substantial direct and indirect costs—but large visible social and corporate gains.

A third problem appears in connection with efforts to apply financial accounting to the measurement of social costs related to corporate inactivity, as when management does not adopt policies and programs that would yield social benefits, on occasion because of considered executive decision, at times through inadvertence or lack of vision. Some of these areas may not even enter management consciousness, of course, although the aggressive representations of special interest activists are rapidly reducing the likelihood of ignorance as a reason for inaction.

A fourth source of difficulty is the absence of clear definition of public expectations of corporate social performance. In recent years these expectations have been expanding, and their ultimate bounds are indeterminate. We confront a set of societal values in transition, with at least the possibility that some of the more extreme claims for social benefits may be significantly modified as their impact on economic costs and prices is broadly recognized.

Still another troublesome conceptual issue is suggested by such a problem as that of the company that chooses to continue operating an obsolete plant in a community in which it is a major employer because closing the facility would inflict severe economic distress on employees and the community. Here economic cost measurements can be specific and precise, but social benefits, or potential social costs, are difficult to handle.

On the technical side, the most obvious difficulty is the fact that many of the measurements cannot be precisely documented in financial terms and must be estimated on the basis of judgments and assumptions. Those skeptical of the feasibility of incorporating social performance measurements within traditional financial accounting systems identify the resulting soft data as a major constraint. An obvious response is that some of the data in corporate financial accounts are also the product of judgments and assumptions. Their indeterminateness does not inhibit their use for decision and control by knowledgeable managers. It is, of course, essential that users of such data understand their provenance and limitations. Such data cannot be conclusive when the administrative requirement is for precise measurement. They have considerable value, however, when their application is in relative measurements of the "more" or "less" character and in setting priorities. A good deal of management information use falls in the relative rather than absolute category. In these circumstances, consistency in measurement can be as helpful as precision for decision and control purposes.

Probably a more substantial practical problem is lack of experience in dealing in financial accounting terms with cost and benefit measures along the full range of corporate social performance. There are no manuals describing tested standard procedures for doing this, and only a sparse professional literature and case inventory on experiments and results. A company that undertakes to apply financial accounting methods to the measurement of social performance decisions and activities will have to innovate. Inevitably, the venture will be open to criticism by those who favor alternative measurement methods and those who doubt the validity of any measurement in these areas.

On balance, the skeptics and critics have a substantive case. Serious conceptual and technical problems need to be resolved in applying financial accounting methods to the measurement of corporate social performance. But the case is even stronger for proceeding to develop the required knowledge, skills, and systems. For internal resource allocation decisions and ongoing program control, and equally for reporting to external publics, management needs measurements in financial and quasi-financial terms.

Most of the conceptual and technical problems can be explored and solutions tested more effectively through practical trial-and-error methods than through speculation and intellectual debate. Corporate managements would find it advantageous to initiate experimental measurement projects, without public announcement or even private commitment to apply the results. The first efforts should be on a limited scale, directed to selected policies and programs that can be quantified (precisely or by estimation) on both cost and benefit sides with existing knowledge and techniques. Areas that require new knowledge and techniques may be reserved for later efforts.

The gains for the company that mounts a serious effort to measure social performance inputs and outputs in financial terms will be substantial. First, there will be a growing inventory of information, improving in quality over time, to facilitate internal decision and control. Second, the data generated will assist reporting on social performance in meaningful terms to shareholders and other publics. Third, as other corporations adopt similar

118

procedures, opportunities will occur for comparing the effectiveness and efficiency of social performance.

The possibility of merging social responsibility accounting and financial accounting within a single comprehensive system clearly is not feasible today and may never be important to accomplish. So much that is useful can be done without getting involved in this ultimate theoretical goal that it is desirable to avoid entanglement in such a thorny bramble.

6

The Responsible Board and the Effective Director

THE performance of boards of directors of large publicly owned corporations has long been a subject for scholarly and popular criticism. Recent developments have stimulated intensified criticism of directors' performance by dramatically illuminating the gap between the law and managerial theories of directors' responsibilities, on one side, and common business practice, on the other.

In a number of well-publicized cases of legal, economic, and moral failure, directors clearly have not fulfilled reasonable trusteeship obligations to shareholders. Reports of these failures have encouraged challenging questions about procedures for selecting outside directors, board structure and agenda, deficiencies in information supplied to outside directors by operating management, outside directors' inability or disinclination to use available information and to identify additional information requirements, and superficial execution of the audit function. Judicial and regulatory rulings have signaled heightened financial risks for directors. Questions are also being raised about the board's role in determining corporate responses to wide-ranging public expectations and demands for new standards and modes of corporate social behavior.

In the view of some observers, many corporate boards have been little more than passive instruments for ritual approval of operating managers' decisions and actions. Only in crisis situations, say some critics, have boards adopted a governance role consistent with their legal and administrative responsibilities. Even then, their actions often have been evaluated as limited to minimal remedial patching and adjusting, with little effort to develop organizational and procedural changes aimed at substantially improving board performance.

Both outside critics and thoughtful practicing managers have advanced proposals for redefining and improving the implementation of traditional board responsibilities and for facilitating constructive board initiatives and responses to emerging challenges to business institutions and their behavior. Specific ideas have been laid on the table in the following areas: appropriate qualifications, competences, and duties of outside directors; active shareholder participation in selection of directors; representation of nonowner interest groups, such as minorities, women, employees, customers, communities, and government; innovations in board structure, organization, and relations with operating management; independent staff support for outside directors; higher and more precise standards for directors' responsibilities for corporate legal, economic, and moral performance; and provision for federal chartering of large corporations.

The proposals offer a grab-bag of constructive suggestions and irrelevancies, as well as some ideas which, if literally applied, might seriously erode the effective functioning of boards. No reasoned assessment of the potential contribution of directors—including areas related to corporate social performance—can fail to recognize, however, that the board is one element in the corporate governance machinery for which change is overdue. Failure by business generally to respond to valid criticism and to present creative initiatives may invite government action.

It would be a gross error to consider these and other possible proposals only in relation to issues of legal compliance or social performance. Most corporate boards have not been organized and used in ways that facilitate their full potential contribution to effective business management aimed at traditional profit objectives. They are fairly characterized as an underutilized, even a wasted management resource. Their performance would deserve examination even if there were no public record of managerial malfeasance, misfeasance, and nonfeasance, and no pressure for new standards of corporate social performance.

The Gap between Concept and Practice

The central issue is the gap between concept and practice. Specifically charged by law with ultimate responsibility for "managing the business" on behalf of shareowners, the typical board has complied with this mandate under conditions that assure minimum interference with the chief executive officer and his senior associates:

1. Contrary to the theory that directors select and remove top management, in common practice it is top management that selects and removes directors. Outside directors, whether a majority or minority of total board

membership, usually are chosen by the chief executive officer and serve at his pleasure. So, of course, do inside directors. The shareowner vote is a ritualized formality which approves an official slate. Most outside directors have business, professional, or social relationships with the chief executive officer. They are not advantageously positioned or motivated to render an objective, independent, and critical evaluation of his performance.

2. The duties and work methods of the board and of individual directors in common practice are not specifically delineated in written mission and job descriptions. What a board does as a whole and what its individual members do are substantially determined by the chief executive officer. He uses this resource as he finds convenient in relation to his view of the needs of the business and his personal management style.

3. The typical board is not involved with corporate plans and strategies in their formative stage. Rather, it receives for formal approval plans that have been prepared by the operating organization, with little opportunity for outside directors to consider alternatives and evaluate comparative trade-offs and risks. The popular guiding precept has been that the board should select capable top management (most simply, a chief executive officer) and support that management without question or interference until it demonstrates its incompetence or untrustworthiness by grossly unsatisfactory performance.

4. Board agendas are usually determined by the chief executive officer and tend to become ritualized. As a result, the business of the board often has more form than content. So long as operating performance and financial condition are satisfactory (which can be roughly defined as not below the "par" of industry averages), there is little

opportunity or encouragement for outside directors to question either ongoing activities or the charted course of the business.

5. The audit responsibility of the board is narrowly conceived and implemented—ordinarily by cursory annual meetings of the audit committee with representatives of the company's public accounting firm, in which summary appraisals are received with respect to the integrity of accounting and financial records and systems. Little or no attention is directed to an audit-type evaluation of corporate policies and programs that are not directly reflected in the accounting records.

6. The typical board membership roster does not include one or several outside directors whose careers, experiences, and interests qualify and motivate them to introduce into board discussions ideas and viewpoints other than those traditionally associated with business management. The tidal movement of a changed set of social attitudes toward corporate behavior has not penetrated many board rooms through the representation of diverse "public" interests by qualified individuals who are encouraged to communicate their knowledge and views.

There are, of course, exceptions to this critical summary. A few corporations for many years have had boards designed, staffed, and motivated to implement fully the concept of ultimate responsibility for managing the business. In a growing but still modest number of large publicly owned companies the revelations and pressures of the last several years have encouraged constructive changes in traditional practices, notably in increasing the number of outside directors, adding women and blacks, and at least minimally strengthening the audit function. In a small number of publicized instances of gross economic, legal, or moral failures by senior line management, outside directors have intervened in critical management areas and, on their own initiative or by direction of a judge or regulatory agency, have begun to design a stronger role and supporting resources for themselves. In these cases—and one may assume in other less critical situations—the actions of outside directors have been stimulated by reports of instituted or threatened stockholder suits. The financial risk that goes with service as a director has become an interesting and sensitive subject.

Sources of Pressures for Change

Publicly owned corporations appear to be in a period of transition from a time when constructive reforms in board structure, membership, agenda, and performance were options open to internal initiatives to a time when, in the absence of such initiatives, major changes are likely to be mandated by governmental action. The advantages of voluntary change are so obvious and substantial that a compelling case can be made for imaginative initiatives by corporate leaders. Voluntary reform can build its designs from specific management experiences, can adapt to specific individual-company needs, can accommodate specific personal relationships and leadership styles. Mandated reform, on the other hand, inevitably would prescribe a degree of uniformity in board structure and operations, greatly weakening the creative flexibility that may be the first requirement for successful governance in a dynamic environment. Beyond this, the introduction of uniform standards, determined and applied from outside the business system, for one element of corporate activity would establish both example and motivation for similar encroachments in other elements. This thrust toward statism can be observed in many areas of public concern, and so can the associated direct costs and indirect constraints on the capacity of private business institutions to maneuver and adapt to change.

Opportunities for business initiatives are suggested by the specific interest groups currently generating pressures for changes in the structure and work of corporate boards. First and foremost are those critics within and friendly to the business system who have called attention to inadequacies in the performance of most corporate boards with respect to their traditional legal responsibilities and their potential contributions to the management of business resources. In the view of these critics, the corporate board—properly manned, organized, and used—can be a valuable top-management resource. It should be put to work within an organizational design that would maximize its contribution. These observers are also concerned that failure to move energetically in this area will invite increasingly severe criticism by less friendly and knowledgeable observers. Such an attack is likely to strengthen demands for mandated changes, with all the unfortunate results public intervention would inevitably introduce.

A second interest group whose criticism of board performance has commanded growing public attention in recent years is composed of those both within and outside the business community who are concerned about general or specific issues associated with the concept of "corporate social responsibility." Both individuals and self-styled "public interest" organizations are asserting the view that boards of directors can be effective influences for change in business behavior in such areas as equal employment and career opportunities, environmental hygiene, safety of work processes and conditions, protection of diverse consumer interests, and contributions to ameliorating a range of community problems. By one device or another, they want to secure effective representation on boards for these constituencies and interests.

Through such representation proponents of change within the business community expect to provide clearer, more direct, more influential expression of changing forces and attitudes in the social environment to which they believe business organizations should be sensitive and, as they find appropriate and feasible, responsive. Proponents of these views outside the business community hope through aggressive representation of constituency interests to force the pace of change in corporate behavior by generating internal pressures that are difficult for operating managers to resist. These critics appear to be indifferent or insensitive to the trade-offs between costs and benefits of specific courses of action, as well as between voluntary initiatives by business and changes mandated by legislative, judicial, and regulatory processes. Disappointed and frustrated by what they regard as dilatory business response to social concerns and needs, they are determined to use the political process to compel reform and are turning with increasing vigor and considerable success to the machinery of our political institutions.

A third source of criticism, currently at a considerably lower level of intensity but with isolated hot points that are likely to intensify and spread, is shareowners, both individual and institutional. The individual shareholder who makes aggressive representations at annual meetings has long been a comic figure for the press, although certainly not for harassed board chairmen. A few such individuals have exerted substantial and, on the whole, constructive influence in stimulating a fuller flow of information to shareholders and more sensitive perception by directors and officers of the rights and interests of owners.

A recent development probably has even greater potential for changing the character and work of the corporate board, however. This is the appearance of organized groups, including institutional as well as individual investors, that advance specific proposals for reform through the proxy process. Their objectives have been diverse, extending to many aspects of corporate performance. Within the diversity have been proposals to change the rules and procedures for selecting and electing candidates for directorships, to provide for some type of constituency representation, to charge boards with explicit responsibility for business behavior in identified areas of social impact and concern, to broaden and deepen the audit function, to provide independent staff support for outside directors, and in various other ways to set standards and goals for board performance and compel reporting of actions and behavior related to such objectives.

Educational, religious, and philanthropic institutions have provided most of the examples to date of investment organizations' participation in this effort to use the proxy process as a change mechanism. It would be reasonable to anticipate, however, that at least some pension funds may join the movement. Other investing institutions may also decide to take a more aggressive attitude toward the managements of companies to which they commit entrusted funds. Recent revelations of board malperformance and the current trend in judicial and regulatory rulings toward defining the trusteeship responsibility

more comprehensively and specifically cannot fail to encourage among all kinds of investing institutions a disposition to apply pressure on management performance by
way of boards of directors.

Finally, a number of special interest groups—women,
minorities, consumers, employees, environmentalists of
various kinds—and numerous subgroups, subcultures,
and splinters within these broad interest categories have
organized themselves as active claimants for protection
of their constituency concerns and redress of perceived
grievances. An emerging goal of many groups is representation on boards of directors for the specific purpose of
advancing the claims of their several constituencies from
within the corporate hierarchy.

A growing, although still small, number of large corporations have brought onto their boards individuals who in
their persons, although clearly not always in their commitments and performance, represent one or another
specific interest group. This development introduces a
critical question. Is the primary function of such directors (1) to sensitize officers and directors to the special
problems, needs, and claims of the interest groups with
which they are intimately familiar by personal association, or (2) to politicize the board by converting it into an
arena in which the traditional commitment to economic
objectives is challenged by and compelled to work out
accommodations with a range of social objectives whose
relationship to economic objectives is often adversary in
the short run, however the two goals may coalesce in the
longer-term future? Defining the desired or appropriate
mission for either special interest communicators or constituency representatives, as the case may be, is both
important and difficult. It directly affects board function,
membership, agenda, organization, working methods,

and relations with operating management. Indirectly, it is bound to influence corporate policies and practices at every economic-social interface.

Separating the Board from Operating Management

The theory that the primary responsibility of directors is to manage the corporation as trusted stewards of the investments of owners—in the specific sense of selecting the chief executive officer and his principal associates, evaluating their performance and removing and replacing them when appropriate, maintaining an informed watch over current business operations, and participating in and approving fundamental resource commitments of material significance to the long-run success of the firm—is rational, necessary, and feasible of implementation. With a very few qualified exceptions, however, American corporate practice related to all aspects of board organization, membership, and work is not consistent with this theory. Furthermore, it can be anticipated that if the visible fault in the governance structure is not repaired by internal business initiatives, changes will be mandated from without through some combination of legislative, regulatory, and judicial actions. The desirability of taking corrective steps to minimize the likelihood of governmental action is not the only reason for considering voluntary reform, of course. At least as important is the case for redesigning the board in the interest of equipping it to fulfill its legal responsibility and deliver its management potential in support of the corporation's basic economic mission.

The first and most important design requirement is to establish the board as an independent and objective element in the corporate structure by separating it from operating management. To put the issue bluntly, there is no serious, rational case, other than the continuance of customary practice, for believing that line managers subordinate in rank to their chief executive officer are competent to render an objective appraisal of their superior's capabilities and performance, or in a position to express a negative judgment if they form one. Nor are senior operating officers, for equally obvious reasons, qualified to assess their own capabilities and performance. Finally, immersed as they are in demanding operating tasks, they are not generally likely to be as sensitive as are at least some types of outside directors to issues related to the changing social environment and their implications for corporate policies and performance.

The inescapable conclusion is that insiders below the rank of chief executive officer have no role as directors and do not belong on the board. They cannot contribute to the implementation of the board's legal or managerial responsibilities. The broad tendency in the past two decades to increase the number of outside directors on major corporate boards—usually, but not always, with a parallel reduction in the number of inside directors—testifies to a growing recognition of the validity of this conclusion. But it is still not uncommon for outside directors to constitute a minority of total board membership. Even the presence of a majority of outsiders does not necessarily respond to the full range of legal and managerial requirements.

The familiar justification for inside directors is the argument that they possess what outsiders lack: the knowledge (and back of the knowledge the experience) required to make properly informed decisions about matters on which the success or failure of an enterprise may depend. This rationalization completely misses the point at issue. It implies that the role of the board is that of a senior operating committee for whose effective functioning an intimate acquaintance with all aspects of ongoing and projected activities is essential.

The overseer function of selecting top managers and appraising all aspects of their performance—including the capabilities, contributions, and compensation of senior officers; the principal strategic thrusts and resource commitments of the enterprise; its financial and moral integrity; the constructive anticipation of potentially critical changes in the external environment and the accommodation of policies and practices to such changes—is different from and substantially unrelated to the operating function. In neither theory nor practice can the overseer or trustee function be performed by those whose capabilities and performance are precisely the objects to which the assessment is addressed. While the analogy to the American Constitution's delineation of a specific check-and-balance system founded on a separation of powers among legislative, executive, and judicial functions should not be pressed too far, it has some instructive relevance in the governance of corporations.

Beyond this, it is not correct to assert, as do some critics of outsider-dominated boards, that the removal of substantial management representation would deprive outside directors of valuable opportunities to become thoroughly familiar with senior managers as a basis for evaluating their qualities in preparation for selecting among candidates for successor top-leadership positions. Outside directors do indeed need to build such knowledge of senior managers. They can readily do this by scheduling frequent opportunities for senior line and staff executives to make formal presentations to the board, respond to directors' questions, and meet informally with board committees and individual directors. In short, a board composed of outside directors can acquire needed operating information possessed by senior managers and can evaluate their capabilities, attitudes, and ideas, without the permanent presence of such managers as fellow directors.

A lively debate can be stirred up with respect to the appropriateness of board membership for a corporation's chief executive officer, currently usually in the position of chairman, occasionally in that of president. Courtney Brown has proposed a complete separation of the work of the board from the work of operating management. His design would specifically designate a chairman of the board who would have no operating responsibilities but would be concerned exclusively with the work of the board, including responsibility for high-level representation of the corporation and its interests before various publics. Only outsiders would serve on this board, with the exception of the chief executive officer.

This strikingly pure and totally logical design is not likely to win the hearts and minds of an overwhelming majority of the current chief executive officers who also chair their boards. This judgment is reinforced by Dean Brown's recommendation that the completely outside board be responsible for selecting its membership, in consultation with the CEO. Complex problems of relationships between the chief operating officer and the chief board officer are inherent in this design. These alone might recommend against its adoption in its pure form, quite aside from the predictable reluctance of most commanding officers to accept curtailment of their range of authority.

One might envision, at least for an interim period, a modification of this design in which the chief executive officer would chair the board but the board would exclude from membership all other operating managers in active service (although the possibility of board membership for retired senior officers would not necessarily be fore-closed). Such a board, particularly one in which authority resided in the outside membership to select its own roster and with the chairman bereft of veto power and his con-tribution limited to suggesting possible candidates, would possess a potential for independence and objectiv-ity limited only by the abilities and motivation of its membership.

Defining the Work of the Board

What most corporate boards do and how they do it (times of actual or incipient crisis always excepted) is the end product of some combination of past practice and the ideas and styles of current chairmen. With only a modest number of exceptions, it is correct to state that the work, organization, and procedures of corporate boards have not been systematically analyzed with a view to develop-ing specific written descriptions of mission, responsibil-ity, and jobs. If a board is to fulfill its legal responsibilities and managerial potential, such an analysis should be undertaken and such written descriptions should be pre-pared. In the course of doing this in the context of an individual corporation's requirements, helpful light is likely to be shed over most of the issues discussed in this chapter, including problems and opportunities at the corporation-society interface and the relation of these matters to corporate strategies, policies, and practices.

If the concept of an outside board objective in posture and independent of management (with or without an independent chairman) is accepted, careful considera-tion should be given to the character and balance of the roster of directors. To establish a fully objective position relative to a corporation's diverse interests, for example, individuals who have materially significant business and professional associations with a company should be explicitly excluded from serving on its board. Such a provision would rule out officers of commercial and investment banks and partners in law firms which regularly provide services to the business, although it would not necessarily deny membership to other bankers and lawyers, whose knowledge and experience would be valuable resources in a diversely representative board. It would also, of course, exclude members of supplier and customer firms.

A more subtle but equally significant issue is the design of a board membership pattern that gives constructive and balanced representation to the range of knowledge, experience, and interests required for thorough implementation of the board's legal and management policy responsibilities. Here the question of constituency representation must be confronted for such interest areas as women, minorities, consumers, communities, and employees. If the prevailing determination is that the mission of such representation is not to subject the board to adversary conflicts among politicized advocates, but rather to sensitize and inform its members about significant environmental forces and issues and through the directors to influence the corporation's social performance, this objective should be clearly expressed in a written description of board mission. It will be necessary, of course, to bring on the board individuals properly qualified to perform such an informational and educational mission who are also disposed to protect and advance the long-run interests of shareowners through a balanced accommodation of economic and social objectives.

The description of board mission and process should make specific provision for the board's prerogative of determining its own committee structure and membership. This power is essential to assure independence and objectivity. It would be unreasonable and unnecessary to deny the chief executive officer the freedom to suggest the names of desirable members or to oppose individual prospects. But it should be made clear in the written description of mission and process that final determination of board organization and membership is a prerogative of the outside directors. They may take such counsel from senior officers as they find appropriate and useful, without relinquishing the decision power.

The independent board should determine its own agenda (without in any way limiting the freedom of operating management to propose content for the agenda). This authority would in normal practice include frequency of meetings of the full board and its standing committees, regular and special subjects, the presence (or absence) of nondirector officers, initiation of requests for special reports, and access to line and staff executives for the board as a whole and for individual directors.

Closely related to the board's control of its agenda is its prerogative of determining the character and detail of operating and financial information supplied to directors. Board members should prescribe the kind of analytical support that accompanies statistical reports. Here, as elsewhere in this description of the structure and work process of the independent board, the objective should be to delineate clearly in both scope and content the board's control over the information flow. This would compel directors to evaluate and specify their information requirements, in contrast to the unfortunate practice in some management-dominated boards of inundating outside directors with a surfeit of data accompanied by inadequate analysis. In general, the independent board should maintain an active rather than a passive posture with respect to its information resources.

Role of the Board in Long-Range Planning

That the board of directors should not become involved in current operations is a principle beyond dispute that is generally respected in business practice. Equally beyond dispute should be the proposition that the board *should* become involved in the long-range planning process. While published research does not indicate how commonly the latter proposition is complied with, post-mortem reports on a series of major business disasters support the conclusion that boards often accept, without probing evaluation, long-range plans recommended by senior operating management. Presumably they do this as part of the pattern of behavior that supports senior operating management as long as it produces satisfactory results.

In contrast to a policy of noninvolvement in current operations, which is appropriately justified by a board's inability to make useful contributions to near-term activities, failure by a board to participate in major long-range decisions involving important resource investments or strategic thrusts is a default of a fundamental board responsibility. Such resource and strategy commitments are the principal substance of long-range plans. They represent, in their final form, the outcome of selection among alternative options with diverse and complex cost-benefit balances. Once approved and activated, such plans may be changed or abandoned only at great expense, in extreme cases adding up to near or actual disaster for the business. Risks of this magnitude are clearly involved in plans that propose major acquisitions or divestments, extensive diversification programs, expansion from national to international operations, or commitment to a new technology. Equally important and just as risk-loaded are future-oriented decisions that reject options of this character. So, too, are plans that incorporate or exclude substantial investment or policy commitments related to sensitive social issues such as environmental pollution, minority employment, or health and safety of the work place.

Directors cannot adequately grasp the implications of long-range resource or policy commitments of this character if they become acquainted with plans only at the final stage when alternatives have been reduced to a single set of recommendations. At something like the semifinal round in the annual planning process, when the principal substantive options with attendant cost-benefit evaluations have reached the level of senior corporate management, provision should be made for reviewing the options with either the full board or a designated board committee. Directors should have an opportunity to question critical assumptions that underlie recommended objectives and strategies, probe critical cost-benefit appraisals, and assess managers' judgments on critical risks. The purpose of this exercise is not to substitute directors' judgment for that of managers, but rather to introduce an objective viewpoint uncommitted to a specific program and unconnected with a particular resource or strategy constituency. By this action, directors will be put in a position to execute a responsibility which they cannot formally evade but which, in the normal long-range planning procedure, they lack knowledge to implement.

Expanding the Board's Audit Function

In a number of recent unsavory reports of management malpractice and questionable morality, directors have taken a narrow and relaxed view of the board's audit function. There can be little doubt that this function requires extensive redefinition for more breadth and depth and vigorous implementation of the enlarged design. More than in most other areas of board activity, the penalties and risks associated with deficiencies in the audit discipline have been identified: in shareowner class action suits, in court decisions, in administrative rules by regulatory agencies, and in proposals for supplemental sanctions and mandated uniform performance standards. Only forthright and widespread voluntary reform by the business community is likely to ward off public control in this area.

In addition to taking a more demanding and rigorous attitude toward the professional standards, methods, and general performance of a corporation's outside public accountants, a responsible board audit committee should satisfy itself that operating management establishes and executes policies and procedures that assure the completeness, accuracy, and integrity of all internal information systems. No publicly owned corporation can afford to permit slack discipline in recording payments to suppliers, or countenance handling off-book transactions outside the formal accounting system. Specific and severe sanctions should be applicable to any employees who violate clearly defined corporate rules, and this regimen should be communicated throughout the organization.

Beyond this, a fully responsible audit committee should evaluate management's implementation of policies and standards of material significance in accomplishing its social performance goals in such sensitive areas as environmental hygiene, personnel administration, consumer interests, and community relations. In implementing this responsibility, such a committee should review the adequacy and accuracy of recording and reporting systems in these areas where in many companies systematic and controlled administration has not been established as institutional routine.

Creating a Board Social Performance Function

Acceptance of a corporate social performance responsibility parallel to and also directly related to the traditional economic performance responsibility will create a need at the board level for a stewardship committee that focuses on this area of company activity. The principal responsibility of this committee should be to sensitize the board to trends in the society's evolving attitudes toward and expectations for the behavior of corporations in general and of their organization in particular. These trends require evaluation and interpretation in relation to the firm's existing and prospective policies and practices.

Board-level committees of this sort, influential in affecting the thinking of fellow directors and senior managers, would surely have reduced the number of reported instances in recent years of failures by some of the largest American companies to bring their personnel policies and practices into line with emerging social concepts of equity in hiring and promoting women and members of minority groups. They would surely have been helpful in minimizing the number of instances of inadequate or slow business response to changing social ideas about protection of consumer interests in such areas as product safety and performance, service policies, credit terms and practices, and advertising. They would surely have encouraged a more forthcoming and more timely response by some giant corporations to public concern about air and water pollution, unhealthy working conditions, and the standards and methods of business-government relations.

In every one of these areas top-management inattention and insensitivity to changing social attitudes and expectations have had damaging results for individual companies and for business as a whole. Major corporations have paid multimillion-dollar penalties and have been subjected to judicial and regulatory rulings governing their future behavior. Some senior executives have narrowly escaped jail. Straitjacketing legislation has been imposed, mandating heavy nonproductive investments by some companies. Possibly even more damaging to the future of the enterprise system, the business community and its leaders have suffered a devastating erosion of public confidence, respect, and credibility which in turn has weakened their ability to win acceptance and support for their constructive initiatives.

The full record clearly demonstrates what a high price has been paid for the failure by many business leaders to understand what is taking place in our society. An issue of this strategic importance deserves attention at the board level.

Independent Staff Support for Outside Directors

The provision of independent staff support for outside directors has at least a superficial appeal to those concerned about the ability of outside directors with necessarily limited time and information resources to identify critical issues, probe them in depth, and retain confidence in the integrity of company staff analyses and conclusions. Such an arrangement would inevitably introduce an adversary posture into relationships between outside directors and operating managers, which could readily politicize the organization. Most experienced senior officers and directors would find the resulting environment an unpleasant environment in which to function under the best of conditions, and in less favorable circumstances a fertile source of distrust and partisan maneuver.

The real need of outside directors for a capability to maintain an active rather than a passive attitude toward senior management probably can be supplied in ways that would be less disturbing to organizational equilibrium. First, there should be clear understanding, confirmed in the board's written "job description," that board committees and individual outside directors have the right to initiate inquiries about any aspects of corporate operations. Second, directors' access to managers subordinate to the chief executive officer should be unrestricted by chain-of-command constraints. And finally, board committees should be empowered to engage outside staff assistance whenever they are dissatisfied with the promptness, comprehensiveness, and accuracy of management's responses to board inquiries. In actual practice, a board's capability to call up such independent staff assistance should go far toward assuring that this extreme action would rarely be found necessary.

An interesting and to some observers more persuasive case can be made for providing outside directors with their own independent legal counsel. The primary consideration is that the interests of outside directors are not identical with those of the chief executive officer and his senior associates. Critical differences are found not only in legal responsibilities defined in statutes and in judicial and regulatory rulings but also in economic and social responsibilities emerging in today's business environment. Without in any way formalizing an adversary position vis-à-vis management, which would be a thoroughly undesirable relationship, the outside directors' mission of objective evaluation defines a need for independent monitoring of ongoing and potential corporate activities in both economic and social areas. Qualified counsel could materially contribute to directors' understanding of their obligations, risks, and opportunities and could assist them in probing areas of policy and operation where their need for information may not be fully matched by operating management's perception of that need.

Responsibility and Effectiveness

One theme underlies this review and evaluation of deficiencies in typical board organization and performance, on one side, and, on the other, proposals for reform and improvement: the board of directors is described as a wasted resource both by those whose sole interest is in improving the quality of corporate management for strictly economic objectives and also by those who, viewing large corporations as powerful social institutions, want to shape their behavior to accommodate social objectives. Many of the improvements in board organization and performance that would assist in satisfying the first group of critics would also create a potential capability for responding to the demands of the second group. Even shareowners who are indifferent to the implications of changing social attitudes toward corporate behavior should be keenly interested in reforming the corporate board to make it fully responsible for the performance of the management it selects to administer the resources of the business, and fully effective in carrying out that responsibility.

Given these dual incentives for reform, the advantages of voluntary initiatives by the business community over changes mandated by legislative, administrative, and judicial actions are clear and substantial.

NOTE: The author is substantially indebted to *Putting the Corporate Board to Work* by Courtney C. Brown (New York: Macmillan Publishing Co., 1976) for the content of this chapter.

7

Top-Management Responsibility for Social Performance

Top corporate management, specifically the chief executive officer and the board of directors, must be responsible for the decision to commit an organization to a philosophy and program of coordinating economic and social performance. This follows from the fact that such a decision will determine the fundamental long-term character of a business and cannot fail substantially to affect its long-term operating results. It will influence the design of the strategic planning system, the allocation of resources, the definition of middle-management assignments together with the standards and procedures for evaluating their performance, personnel policies and practices, and almost every other aspect of the total operation of the business. For all these reasons, the decision charts a new course for a firm and inescapably is the prerogative and the duty of its commanding officer, under instruction or approval by its board of directors.

This policy decision would be an empty action, however, unless accompanied by a fully developed plan for its execution. Where that plan involves, as in this instance it clearly does, radical innovation in business philosophy that will be viewed by many subordinates as breaking with traditional management doctrine, the chief executive officer and his senior associates bear a special responsibility. They must both articulate principle and supply example. They must instruct, persuade, and counsel. They must think through and engineer adaptations in organization structure, motivation, and operating systems that will facilitate the transition to a new way of corporate life. By statement and action they must overcome skepticism, inertia, even opposition grounded in perceived self-interest. All of this raises practical problems well beyond those involved in the fundamental policy commitment. If not thoroughly analyzed in advance of the policy decision, they are likely to expose the chief executive officer to charges of hypocrisy or cosmetic public relations arising within and outside the organization. If many major corporations are perceived by the public to be vulnerable to such criticism, the general decline of confidence in the business system and the parallel deterioration of the credibility of business leaders, both so marked in recent years, will be reinforced to a degree that will make restoration of trust extremely difficult.

Integrated Responsibility for Comprehensive Social Performance

The unqualified necessity for an integrated approach by top-level line management to all aspects of a company's social performance is documented by frequently observed deficiencies of fragmented approaches to the issue. A number of companies during recent years have initiated piecemeal social performance programs and activities designed to deal with specific problems and opportunities identified by top management as in some way important to its organization's operating success or public image. Some firms, for example, have singled out employment of minorities as a special object of attention and have created such a position as "manager of minority relations" or "urban affairs officer," usually under the administrative jurisdiction of a staff vice president with broad responsibility for personnel relations or public and governmental relations. Some companies have identified for special attention the development of minority-owned suppliers of products and services and have designated a staff position with a mission to encourage and monitor procurement from such suppliers. In some organizations the primary interest has been in reducing environmental pollution or upgrading hygiene and safety of work place and work process, and staffing has reflected this emphasis. In some, the focal issue has been improved consumer relations, again with designation of a staff officer with special responsibility for formulating relevant policies and programs.

However well intentioned and whatever their accomplishments, all of these and other fragmented efforts of individual corporations to respond to perceived social performance problems or opportunities exhibit common deficiencies on both conceptual and operating levels. On the conceptual level, the fragmented approach encourages senior managers to regard each specific program as a self-sufficient response to a special societal requirement or need. This reduces the likelihood that corporate leaders will recognize and evaluate the emergence of a

147

new environment for business formed by a comprehensive and interrelated set of performance expectations. The result is a continual lag in grasping the full meaning of emerging governing conditions for the business system. At least as important is the fact that a top management that has not clarified its own perception of what is happening in our society will not be able to perform the essential task of orienting and educating middle managers, from whose ranks will come the next generation of leaders.

This conceptual deficiency has obvious operating implications. It discourages introducing social performance considerations into the strategic planning process. It gets in the way of any effort to anticipate the effects of evolving public attitudes. Instead, it commits the organization to the familiar syndrome of resisting change and responding to mandated performance with minimal compliance. It fails to illuminate the necessity for revising the duties and responsibilities of middle managers and for adapting performance evaluation systems and related motivational machinery to their enlarged operating assignments. It handicaps efforts to develop meaningful cost-benefit analyses. Above all, it instills throughout the organization a sense of defensive and grudging accommodation to unreasonable and undesirable restrictions, which handicap management's ability to execute its primary mission of maximizing traditional economic performance.

A particular difficulty with fragmentation is its damaging influence on organization structure and behavior. Each special program is usually assigned to a discrete staff function within an established administrative activity group. Staff specialists have the task of developing policies, standards, and procedures, and then working through dotted-line organizational relationships to persuade operating managers to accept and implement the program.

Line managers inevitably face conflicts between traditional economic performance objectives and new social performance objectives. Since established objectives are associated, in line managers' perceptions and equally in reality, with performance evaluation and the associated reward-penalty system, managers' judgments about relative priorities tend to subordinate the new social programs to what they perceive as their primary goals. Often the confusion is compounded by competition among social programs for line managers' attention and by conflicting claims on available resources. Requests for guidance and adjudication that move up the authority hierarchy are received by senior line officers (departmental, geographic, functional) who themselves have no explicit social performance responsibilities but do have explicit economic performance responsibilities. The resulting decision problems are rendered even more complicated when managers are under pressure to accomplish short-term results, as is usually the case. Most social programs have quite visible short-run costs and, subject to traditional performance criteria, much less visible long-run pay-offs.

At the same time, the absence of a clearly articulated commitment by the chief executive officer to specific performance objectives, supported by a direct assignment of responsibility to subordinate senior line officers to accomplish the identified objectives and accompanied by guidance on priorities applicable in conflict situations, invites skepticism about all aspects of social performance. Those disposed to be hostile toward what they see as subversion of corporate purpose or, even worse, a general attack on the integrity of the private enterprise system are subjected to neither persuasion nor restraint. In such a situation, it is easy and attractive for critics to point out how hiring and promoting blacks and women raise costs and disturb the morale and security of existing employees; how investing in pollution control yields no productive output and diverts money from profitable plant modernization and expansion; how modification of marketing practices to satisfy the complaints of consumer activists threatens competitive market position and shrinks operating margins.

This type of criticism is hard to rebut in a company in which the chief executive officer has not established his personal commitment to social performance. It is likely to be especially destructive of the kind of rational analysis of complex accommodations and trade-offs among economic and social objectives that is essential for an effective long-range program. In such a hostile atmosphere, it is inevitable that most managers will view staff-supported social policies and programs as peripheral matters, secondary to the "real work" of the business, at best worth only minor attention in the context of mainstream operations.

In effect on long-run corporate performance, however, none of these deficiencies of the piecemeal approach is as dangerous as the way it limits imaginative analysis of the full array of available strategic options. By focusing on one issue at a time, it encourages managers to think defensively, respond to rather than anticipate external pressures, and ignore opportunities for taking initiatives alone or in concert with other private or public organizations. In particular, it fails to draw management attention to emerging situations in which the individual firm or the business community can recommend constructive proposals that would serve the public interest without creating unwieldy administrative bureaucracies or public management systems that are open invitations to inefficiency or corruption. The public inertia and restricted social imagination of many corporate leaders have been responsible for their generally limited participation in designing solutions to the urgent problems of our society, not any restriction of their access to political institutions. Activist leaders representing nonbusiness interests have been influential because they were sensitive to areas of growing dissatisfaction and aggressive in proposing legislative and regulatory solutions. Examples of precisely this experience can be found in every area of significant discontent with business social performance.

Requirements for Effective Management of Social Performance

The first requirement for effective management of corporate social performance is therefore a clear signal to his organization by the chief executive officer of personal responsibility for the decision to put social objectives on a par with economic objectives in managing the business. This commitment must be communicated by precept and example to all managers. Only through such a demonstration can the corporate leader persuade skeptics and opponents and influence established patterns of thought and behavior. Anything less will be appraised as "high-level public relations" in the pejorative sense of that abused term.

One of the most effective ways for the CEO to demonstrate the integrity of his commitment is to take the lead in redesigning the composition, organization, and agenda of the board of directors. Important reinforcing evidence would be adaptation of the strategic planning process to incorporate social projections, and the issuance of planning guidelines that include social as well

151

as economic performance objectives. Very few skeptics would remain in the management group if, in addition, the CEO directed the revision of written descriptions of senior and middle managers' duties and responsibilities to include social performance standards in terms appropriate for each position, and if he further provided for evaluation of managers' performance against these standards.

Administrative responsibility for social performance should not be delegated to a senior officer reporting to the CEO. The destabilizing effect of such a delegation is suggested by the simple reminder that a company's economic performance is always viewed as every manager's responsibility within the blueprint of a comprehensive planning and operating scheme. A company's social performance must rest on an equally broad base. Charging an individual senior official with planning and managing social performance would be inconsistent with this philosophy and would encourage other managers at senior and middle levels to feel less than full responsibility for establishing and achieving social performance objectives within their chains of command.

A second requirement is for the chief executive officer and his principal management associates to define the meaning of social performance in the specific context of the company's production and marketing processes, the geographic scope of its operations, employment conditions and employees' attitudes and expectations, competitive conditions and dynamics, and the circumstances and inherent obligations of its community and customer relationships. The concepts involved in such a definition will be novel to many managers. What is called for, however, parallels the familiar standards of economic performance that are laid down by the leadership of every well-managed corporation, for its own guidance and as benchmarks for planning and evaluation throughout the organization.

Long incorporated in planning and operating practice, guidelines for economic performance (such as rate of growth, level of profitability, return on invested capital, and scope of approved business activity) are routinely accepted and applied by senior and middle managers in mature firms. Only on the relatively rare occasions when substantial changes in technological or economic circumstances require review and revision of established economic standards are most managers made aware of the complex considerations involved in formulating standards qualitatively and quantitatively within acceptable and feasible limits. The difficulties that will be encountered in creating for the first time comparable standards for social performance will be greater than those dealt with in setting initial economic benchmarks only because of managers' relative inexperience and lack of training in thinking in social performance terms and the absence of a language of description and measurement with which managers are familiar and comfortable. These are indeed substantial difficulties, but they are not in any sense overwhelming. Moreover, management really has no alternative other than the thoroughly unattractive passive acquiescence in the creation by ignorant or hostile nonbusiness interests of a radically transformed environment for the business system that will endanger its survival.

A chief executive's definition of social performance objectives in specific terms that parallel and are coordinated with the company's economic goals will help to resolve a predictable initial difficulty. There is persuasive current evidence that the leaders of large corporations as a class are well ahead of their own middle managers in perceiving the social drift and its implications for business. To the extent that this gap exists in any organization, the initial reception through management ranks of a newly articulated fundamental posture toward the firm's social performance is likely to be one of acute disorientation, reflecting some mixture of skepticism, disbelief, misunderstanding, confusion, and even hostility. Many managers will not grasp what the boss is talking about, why he is concerned with societal issues, how the new viewpoint and related expressed or implied policies will translate into operations, or what the impact will then turn out to be on the responsibilities and duties of individual managers.

The best way to reduce and ultimately eliminate this confusion is to convert concept to practice as promptly as possible. This can be done most effectively by talking about specific aspects of business behavior, specific standards of performance, specific changes in managers' jobs, and specific procedures for evaluating managers' execution of their new responsibilities and duties. The description of these specifics is likely to be most credible if the underlying considerations are perceived to be pragmatic, if the limits of feasible corporate action are clearly identified, if the commitment to play an aggressive and constructive role in the social and political process is strongly asserted, and if managers are assured of top-level support and assistance in handling the multitude of operational difficulties and frictions they can realistically anticipate in the initial phases of change.

Defining Social Performance Concepts

The chief executive has the task of defining the concepts of social performance that are relevant for his company in terms of a three-dimensional matrix. The first dimension is concerned with varieties of areas for business activity. At one end of the array are actions that must be taken because they are mandated by law or regulation pursuant to law from which there clearly is no recourse or reason to seek recourse. Most fair employment actions, but probably only a small proportion of other social performance actions, will be appraised as unquestionably within this category.

At the other extreme are social performance programs urged by ignorant or naive reformers, and occasionally by ideological opponents of the market system. These proposals deserve vigorous opposition by business leaders and business institutions. Their implementation would weaken the market system, limit the ability of the economy to grow by applying crippling constraints on incentives to invest in expansion of the resource base, or compel business to commit resources under conditions of grossly disadvantageous cost-benefit balances. Examples of issues in this category are price or margin controls in circumstances other than national security emergencies; pure air standards whose attainment is feasible only by halting energy expansion or curtailing economic activity and related employment; and expansion of the public sector (as in social security, medical, and welfare benefits) in such scope, scale, and timing as to destroy business and individual incentives by overloading the tax structure or cause a rate of general inflation that would eviscerate the nation's financial integrity and public confidence in the society's future.

Between these extreme categories where the need for positive or negative action is obvious are two areas that deserve more subtle analysis. Here are found most of the difficult problems of strategic choice. The first area includes possible actions that are supported by strong and growing social pressure though not yet mandated by law or administrative order. The lesson of relevant history is unmistakable. In a political democracy, interest groups that express vigorous concern about specific perceived problems are likely to achieve the legislative resolution they propose unless other interest groups are equally vigorous in their opposition and also act either to remove the underlying problems or to propose attractive alternative solutions.

From prohibition of alcoholic beverages to protection of consumers this scenario has played itself out repeatedly. In the business interest—in the larger sense also in the national interest—corporate leaders must understand that simple opposition to ill-considered and dangerous proposals designed to cope with problems that have captured substantial public attention is rarely a winning strategy. Even worse, continued opposition unaccompanied by alternative solutions communicates to a large share of the affected public the message that the business interest is opposed to the broader public interest.

Examples of issues in this category, past and present, are easily identified. The nation's welfare and health care systems in all their grossly inefficient and ineffective technical and economic terms are what they are in good part because the business and professional communities opposed clumsy solutions to serious public needs advanced by other interests, while concurrently failing to design and fight for more efficient and effective alternatives. A widely held public view is that business has been unreasonable and even irresponsible in its opposition to schemes for cleansing the air and water environment of the pollution to which industry has been a major contributor. The result has been, on one side, a dangerous failure to educate the public about the real costs of pushing environmental hygiene to its theoretical limits, and, on the other, absence of any organized effort to study the relative effectiveness of the variety of possible administrative approaches to cleansing the environment—such as performance specifications, user charges, tax remission, and others—each of which might be particularly appropriate in a unique company or industry situation. The confusing and costly jungle of existing and potential government actions to protect consumer interests is largely a product of the failure of business leadership to understand and articulate the fundamental identity of business and consumer interests. The perceived passivity and indifference of business to consumers' complaints created opportunities for consumer activists to lobby successfully for legislative and regulatory solutions. These needs should never have been allowed to continue unserved by the business community.

The other intermediate category involves areas where there may be special constraints on particular social performance actions under consideration by corporate officers. These constraints, while not necessarily binding in all circumstances, may be substantial enough to justify careful exploration of the limits of maneuver and the indirect costs or political disadvantages that may be associated with the constraints. Of special concern here are union and employee relations in the context of some aspects of nondiscriminatory promotion policies (particularly in implementing affirmative action programs designed to correct or compensate for prior discrimination); community relations in the context of environmental and plant hygiene policies and programs; and trade relations in the context of consumer protection policies and programs.

The second dimension of the matrix is concerned with distinctions among social performance actions that are feasible for one company; actions that, while not feasible for one company, are or may be feasible for a group of companies (in a single industry or locality); and actions that require governmental sponsorship or direct legislative or regulatory intervention, to which business managers can contribute valuable technical or administrative guidance. In contrast to the first dimension, which lays out options with respect to what social performance actions may be feasible, this dimension identifies choices with respect to who can or should act.

Distinctions among single-company, multicompany, and governmental social performance actions should be drawn in terms of practical operational considerations. In general, the individual corporation should take a positive approach to opportunities for improving its social performance subject to the constraint that no commitment should be made to policies or programs that would be likely to have a significant adverse effect on either profitability or competitive position. Where this constraint is appraised as operative for one company but not for a group of companies in the same industry or geographic area, it is advantageous, in preference to the alternative of governmental intervention in response to interest group pressure, for management to explore the feasibility of securing voluntary coordinated action by a relevant group of companies. Where coordinated action is not feasible, because of either antitrust restrictions or the reluctance of potential collaborators to take voluntary initiatives in concert, and where there is also a strong probability of some kind of governmentally mandated action, it is advantageous for informed business leaders to make a vigorous effort to contribute to the technical and administrative design of the proposed legislative or regulatory action.

The strategy underlying the general decision rule favors voluntary action by business over government-mandated action. Where voluntary action is judged not to be feasible for cost or other reasons and where analysis of social needs and expectations indicates a substantial probability of governmental action, the strategy favors constructive participation by business in designing the structure, standards, and procedures of prospective legislation or regulation. The strategic objective is to demonstrate and implement the concern and involvement of business in the public interest by contributing to the development of effective and efficient solutions to serious social problems.

There is a simple rationale for business commitment to this strategic objective. While the modern industrialized economy has made enormous contributions to the physical well-being of its host society, it has also created real and perceived wounding side effects—physical, social, and psychic. In addition, the advance of living standards for most people to a state of comfort, if not of affluence, has stimulated interest in the quality of life. The business community in general and the leaders of major corporations in particular have been perceived and portrayed as generally insensitive or indifferent to the side effects of industrialization. Often they have stubbornly opposed efforts to ameliorate what are judged by many to be serious social problems. In effect, they have permitted the business interest to be identified as different from, even opposed to, the general social interest, as well as the specific interests of significant and politically powerful elements in the society.

This widening gap goes far to explain the growing distrust of corporate leaders. It also helps to explain the failure of well-intentioned business efforts to use education and advertising to build understanding and respect for the enterprise system. These communications programs have not been productive because they have not addressed the causes of public disaffection. The central problem is not popular hostility to or ignorance about the business system. It is discontent with some of the system's behavior and, more broadly, with some of the effects of advanced industrialization in an affluent society. When business is seen as directly concerned about conforming its behavior to societal expectations and ameliorating or removing the wounding side effects, it can be anticipated with some confidence that business institutions and their leaders will experience a rising trend of public respect and trust.

The third dimension of the matrix is, of course, time. The evolving social climate for business must be tracked far enough in advance of the development of strong pressures for specific changes in corporate behavior to allow time for consideration of the desirability and feasibility of voluntary initiatives. Most companies have a poor record for anticipating important public pressures for changed social performance. Strong demands for legislation and regulation in the areas of fair employment, environmental pollution, consumer protection, and safety and hygiene of the work place have surprised business leaders repeatedly. This failure of vision has forced corporations into a reactive posture, has limited their flexibility and reduced their options in accommodating to public expectations, and has contributed to the general perception of business as an adversary of the public interest. It has also severely constrained the ability of the business community to influence the development of public attitudes about corporate social performance and the design of remedial legislation and regulation.

The familiar and sensible management commitment to a policy of "no surprises" in the economic area needs to be extended to the total business environment. The best way to do this for all management ranks is to incorporate social performance within the strategic planning system. This will create a demand for forecasting trends in public attitudes and for early warning on issues likely to surface as important objects of public concern. It will also encourage managers with planning responsibilities to assess the meaning of anticipated social developments for their own business, for their industry, and for business in general. As this practice enters the planning system, it will help to build a foundation for identifying significant opportunities and problems, and for distinguishing among situations favoring individual company action, those favoring cooperative action, and those in which some type of governmental action may be desirable or necessary.

Senior Management Participation in Social Performance Decisions

In formulating a comprehensive set of social performance policies and programs, the chief executive officer will find it helpful to draw on all elements of his senior management structure for information and counsel. The process of doing this systematically will generate important secondary benefits. It will sensitize the group to the meaning and importance of the commitment to coordinating social and economic objectives for the whole organization. As senior executives share a common understanding of the compelling reasons for the commitment, perceive its application throughout the organization, and contribute to the design of implementing policies and programs, their sense of responsibility for translating the commitment into operational reality will be strengthened. This attitude will be transmitted, in turn,

161

to middle managers in terms that will help to counter whatever skepticism or hostility may exist among those who make the system work day by day.

The chief executive's first resource should be—and if properly constituted will be—his board of directors. Strengthened by outside directors whose combined experience and knowledge encompass business, government, and a variety of other interests, the board can influence the chief executive officer's concern with corporate social performance in several valuable ways. This assistance will be most effectively focused if a special board committee is created with particular responsibility for proposing, monitoring, and evaluating social performance policies and programs in relation, on one side, to the opportunities and challenges generated by the evolving environment, and, on the other side, to the effectiveness and efficiency of internal resource utilization. Such a committee can provide the chief executive with a balanced perspective of relationships between society and business and objective appraisals of specific pressures on the company and its industry. It can address discerning questions about proposed corporate social performance initiatives and equally about failures to act in circumstances that seem to require or favor action. It can sustain the chief executive's confidence in the correctness of his chosen course when he encounters disaffection from operating associates or from the leaders of other business organizations. Finally, its official endorsement of his comprehensive social performance strategy will help to rebut any criticism that may arise from some shareholders.

All senior line and staff officers have valuable knowledge and experience to contribute to the chief executive officer's definition of a concept of social responsibility that is relevant and feasible for their company. In calling on their help he will gain two important additional benefits. First, responsibility for determining social performance objectives and strategies will be identified as part of the job of every officer. Second, as a result of sharing in establishing goals and formulating programs for their accomplishment, all senior officers will be committed to delivering the necessary operating results through their organizational structures. This all-hands commitment is essential to break down the indifference, skepticism, and hostility that are predictable reactions in management groups whose leaders are not personally associated with activities that many executives perceive as tangential, even disadvantageous, to their primary duties.

The senior planning officer should carry primary responsibility for developing the conceptual, analytical, and procedural system required to facilitate integrated planning for economic and social objectives through all organizational levels that participate in the planning process. One of his primary tasks is to identify the areas and activities at the interface between the company and its environment where social performance pressures have been or are likely to be experienced. In multiproduct firms with numerous manufacturing facilities, there may be a substantial number and variety of such pressure points. In a multinational company, cultural differences add a further complication through their disparate influence on the presence and intensity of issues of public concern.

The planning officer must evaluate these issues and determine their relative importance and urgency, in view of projected general public and interest group attitudes and actions, on one side, and internal company policies and programs, on the other. From this information base he must provide both general planning guidelines for all line officers with planning responsibilities (parallel, in effect, to the broad economic guidelines that serve a similar planning foundation function), and "alert and early warning" notices to his senior-management colleagues in charge of other business functions.

In addition to general planning guidelines, managers responsible for formulating plans require assistance in extending their competence in analyzing social performance issues and in coordinating social and economic objectives and strategies within their areas of responsibility. Planning procedures also need examination and appropriate redesign to assure comparability of information in the content of plans as they move upstream through organization levels and to facilitate aggregation at divisional and corporate levels. In a corporation with an established formal strategic planning system, analytical and procedural methods applicable to general economic and market trends are well understood by the management team. There is likely to be considerable uncertainty, however, in handling social trends, attitudes, and pressures, and at least initial difficulty in bringing to these considerations comparable thoroughness and uniformity of treatment.

The senior officer for the production function—at the corporate or the divisional level, depending on the organization structure—will be the chief executive's primary source of information and counsel on opportunities, costs, and investment requirements associated with social performance issues in manufacturing. The principal areas where public concern about business behavior has been most visible include degradation of the external environment (notably in befouling air, water, and terrain, but recently gaining in importance for some industries have been noise and odors, and for certain locations the aesthetic appearance of production facilities); safety and hygiene of work place and process; and a number of aspects of product design as they determine effectiveness and efficiency of product performance, durability, safety, service and repair, and for some products, energy use. Some additional areas of possible future public concern have been identified by observers of social trends: geographic location (with both positive and negative aspects), seasonal and cyclical continuity of operations, and the social aspects of the work experience (job enrichment, employee participation in decisions about work process, job assignments, and scheduling).

This is a complex menu of opportunities and problems. The experiences and experiments of some companies have already indicated that in many of these areas opportunities can be found for simultaneously responding positively to social expectations and demands and also realizing economic gains through cost reductions, heightened productivity, or more efficient use of resources. It is equally clear, of course, that in every area satisfaction of external pressures may significantly raise costs, require substantial (sometimes prohibitively large) investment, and exert a negative influence on productivity. Furthermore, there is no uniformity among companies in the economic results that are likely to follow any specific strategic approach in any area cited. Circumstances alter cases with a vengeance, and "it all depends" must be the starting point for all analyses. This confusing situation suggests the importance of the contribution of information and counsel that the chief executive requires from his senior production officer before determining a desirable and feasible set of social performance strategies.

A comparable mixed array of opportunities and problems is found in the marketing function. Among all the areas in which new public demands and expectations for changes in corporate social performance have appeared in recent years, concern for better protection of consumer interests and for improved service of consumer needs and wants has claimed a dominant share of media attention. Powerful and politically sophisticated organizations now represent consumer interests, applying pressure on both business and governmental organizations, and also on communications media. At the same time, the range of issues in which individual consumers and consumer organizations and activists are interested has broadened. From an early focus on assuring product and related service performance consistent with product and service claims, the general consumer movement has expanded to include product safety, pricing practices, advertising practices (not simply truthful and full disclosure but also terms of advertising to children), clarity of financing arrangements, nondiscriminatory treatment of all categories of consumers (as in extension of credit and other financial services to minorities and women), and other concerns. In the broadest sense, what is occurring might be described as a transformation from an earlier focus on the citizen as consumer to a current focus on the consumer as citizen. This transformation is illustrated by the active intervention of consumer groups in such issues as licensing of atomic power facilities, regulation of strip mining of coal, and control of automobile tailpipe emissions, to cite only a few of many available examples.

As in the production function, changing public attitudes toward corporate behavior in the marketplace should not be viewed as inevitably hostile to business interests. If the primary purpose of any business is to satisfy customer needs and wants and the primary challenge to management is to discover how to do this more effectively and more profitably than competitors, then sensitivity to and concern for evolving consumer interest are surely in the mainstream of marketing management. It can only be gross strategic error for any business to allow itself to be perceived as an adversary of consumers and their interests. The fact that surveys of consumers' assessments of their own experiences as buyers and users of products and services have repeatedly indicated substantial dissatisfaction is a measure of the inability of many business leaders to understand the realities of supplier-customer relationships. Much of the organized consumer movement can be traced directly to the insensitivity and carelessness of business.

It follows that many of the adaptations of policy and strategy required to bring corporate behavior in the marketplace into conformity with consumer expectations and demands represent opportunities rather than threats. The senior marketing officer can be a valuable source of information and counsel to the chief executive officer on current and projected developments among customers and consumer groups. Some of these situations will clearly be open for advantageous exploitation by a single company, with sales and margin gains well in excess of any incremental costs involved in product, service, and marketing adjustments. In other circumstances, single-company initiatives may be evaluated as competitively disadvantageous. Here the optimal strategy may be collective action (where feasible in the context of legislative or regulatory constraints) or business proposals for governmental remedy of substantial consumer problems for which voluntary solutions are not forthcoming.

However reluctant some corporate executives may be to recommend governmental solutions for market problems, they must come to recognize that no amount of communicating to citizens the achievements and benefits of private industry will persuade millions of consumers that they are well served by business when their personal buying and using experiences make them critical of the way they perceive themselves to be treated.

167

That much of the problem can be traced to a minority of business organizations will not, unfortunately, materially change the predictable outcome. Consumers, whose consciousness of their market and political power has been extraordinarily raised in recent years, will insist on the removal of their major discontents, if not by business voluntarism and self-policing, then by governmental mandate.

The chief executive will look to his senior personnel officer for counsel on policies, strategies, and timing in the areas of fair employment, and employee and manager education and training programs related to both the introduction of nondiscriminatory administration of hiring and promotion decisions, and the effective use of women and minorities in assignments that are new to them and that other members of the organization are not used to seeing them in. These are sensitive areas where it is easier to determine what should be done for moral reasons (and, because of laggard business initiatives, for legal reasons as well) than it is to carry policy into operations against contractual or traditional seniority practices and the institutionalized folkways of white male supervisory and managerial groups.

The senior officer responsible for research and development can provide information and counsel with respect to product and process innovations that are related to social performance. In the product area may be found opportunities for enhancing product safety, durability, and ease of service and repair, as well as opportunities for changes in design to conform more closely to evolving customer preferences. The recent experience of the automobile industry offers familiar examples of such opportunities, and also of challenges to develop new technology to meet higher standards of fuel conservation and emission control. That experience also illustrates the costs, time lags, and market problems that have complicated management's responses and enmeshed the industry in governmental legislative and regulatory constraints. In the process area research has opportunities (always accompanied by costs and risks) for developing technology applicable to pollution control, commercial utilization of contaminating wastes, and safety and hygiene of the work place. For all of the above areas the chief executive needs professional counsel in determining the potentials and limits of corporate policies aimed at anticipating and responding to expectations and demands for improved social performance.

The senior financial officer is uniquely positioned to identify and evaluate the revenue and cost implications of social performance action and inaction throughout the business. His conclusions on the financial results, near-term and long-term, of socially oriented decisions must strongly influence—although not always ultimately determine—the policy, strategy, and action program decisions taken by the chief executive officer and the board of directors. There will, of course, be situations in which nonfinancial considerations will govern the corporate course. To the extent that profit implications are clearly laid out, however, the range within which other considerations enter will be both curtailed and specifically defined, and the coordination of economic and social performance will be more rationally accomplished.

The foregoing description of the extent to which the chief executive officer can and should draw his senior-management associates into the process of formulating relevant and feasible social performance concepts and programs emphasizes the comprehensive impact on a business of adapting its operations to the new social contract. It also suggests the inadvisability of assigning to a single corporate officer responsibility for evaluating and proposing policies and strategies that enter as positive and negative factors in every organization function, with complex interactions and potential influence on the long-term posture of the business.

8

Middle-Management Responsibility for Social Performance

THE environment within which middle managers work differs from the senior-management environment in a number of important ways. The motivational influences that act upon middle managers are not the influences that act on top executives. Middle managers have a direct exposure to operating problems in factory, marketplace, and office from which top managers are usually shielded except at times of crisis. The decisions that determine middle managers' short-term income and status and their long-term career prospects are based on different performance criteria than those applicable to senior managers. Middle managers see the organizational structure within which they function from a different viewpoint, which determines how they assess its authority hierarchy and its political interplay. They are at a different stage in their life cycles than their superiors,

171

with different family responsibilities and different relationships with their communities. In effect, the entire
complex of experiences to which they are exposed on and
off the job is different from the experience network of top
management.

The net of all these influences is to encourage among
middle managers a set of attitudes that uniquely determines their behavior, their perception of job responsibilities, and their responses to changes in organizational
policies and programs. These attitudes can generally be
described as strongly career-oriented, attuned to economic rather than social performance, highly sensitive to
formal short-term performance measurements, focused
on self more than on organization, and disposed to encourage viewing managerial career progression as influenced by job performance and organizational politics.

How most middle managers appraise the concept of
corporate social performance is powerfully determined by
these attitudes. So, too, is how they perceive and evaluate
statements of corporate policy related to social performance, and how they respond to and implement social
performance programs that impinge (or are perceived to
impinge) on their duties and responsibilities. This is a
critical relationship. It suggests that, with the exception
of a few middle managers who, for reasons of nature or
nurture, may be particularly sensitive to changing social
expectations for corporate behavior, the determining
frame of reference for the typical middle manager is the
perceived effect of any corporate social performance policy or program on his career.

There are, of course, middle managers who clearly see
what is happening at the business-society interface.
Some of these managers probably welcome the changes
in corporate behavior that have occurred and that they
anticipate will occur either voluntarily or under public

mandate. It is unlikely, however, that more than a few middle managers will accept and vigorously implement such changes within their own administrative purview unless the organizational determinants of their attitudes and behavior are reengineered to provide positive motivation for them so to act.

Those in corporate leadership positions who want to introduce social performance objectives as a coordinate of economic performance objectives must thoroughly understand this motivational issue. Senior officers of a number of companies in recent years had a relevant experience when they introduced formal long-range planning in an organization in which middle managers perceived the reward-penalty system as closely tied to short-run operating results measured by annual profit, sales, cost, and return-on-assets budgets. Beneath managers' superficial compliance with the numerical formalities of the annual planning exercise primary attention continued to be directed to maximizing short-run results. Managers resisted making investments or incurring costs aimed at strengthening the base for long-term performance if they believed such commitments would significantly depress short-term operating results. They did this even while acknowledging privately their awareness that their decisions would probably create future problems. In their judgment, the signals emanating from the perceived reward-penalty system reported the real interest of top management more accurately than those suggested by the newly introduced planning procedure.

Determining Influences for Middle Managers' Behavior

If a manager's behavior is largely determined by his assessment of the factors he perceives as most influential in promoting his career, any effort by his superiors to modify that behavior must start by defining those factors and evaluating their relative importance. Research and operating experience indicate that five factors, present in every manager's organizational environment, override all other behavior-influencing considerations. They are highly visible to the manager, for himself and also for his peers. They are the center of attention when managers appraise their prospects, alone or in the company of their associates.

The first is the manager's job description—the formal definition of the responsibilities and duties of the position he occupies, his line of reporting to the next higher organizational level, his authority span over lower levels, and his coordinating relationships across organizational boundaries. This charter serves as the primary blueprint for his general field of action. However, since it is usually drafted in the most comprehensive language and rarely indicates the relative importance of the several elements of the job assignment, the manager must look elsewhere for necessary guidance on what to emphasize and how to implement his top priorities.

The second factor is the manager's perception of the specific performance goals and standards used by superiors in appraising his implementation of assigned duties and responsibilities. In almost all organizations these criteria are expressed in the unit budget. It matters little (in effect on behavior, not necessarily in effect on attitude and morale) whether a manager participates in formulating his unit's budget or has it imposed by higher authority. In either case, the officially approved budget is the visible benchmark. It becomes the performance commitment. It determines priorities of management attention and action. In some organizations, the operating budget may be supplemented by certain nonoperating commitments of a formal written character covering such areas as recruiting, training, and development of subordinates. When present, these goals command attention, although it is usually subsidiary to the attention given to operating objectives. If operating or time pressures squeeze a manager, activities related to the secondary goals tend to be curtailed.

Even explicit budget objectives require additional refinement and reinforcement as a guide to a manager's behavior, since most budgets contain component elements with trade-off relationships: more of one element can be secured by accepting less of another. This needed refinement and reinforcement is provided by the third factor—the formal performance measurement system that defines the budget items for which performance is specifically measured and the time frame to which measurement is applied. This information may be adequately communicated to a manager by the detailed schedule that compares results attained with budget objectives for intermediate periods within the budget period and at its conclusion. If the budget and periodic measurement of performance are laid out in complex detail, however, the significant clues to which a manager is sensitive are provided by his perception of the specific budget and performance items that regularly arouse his superiors' greatest interest, the items for which above- or below-budget performance regularly generates praise or criticism.

The fourth factor is the manager's perception of the organization's reward-penalty system, in its official description and as he observes its application to himself and his peers. If the official description is at variance with the observed application pattern, it is, of course, the latter that captures credibility. The intervening gap is ascribed to the working of the organization's political system,

175

which then, as the fifth factor, becomes the object of particularly intense analysis directed at developing a degree of understanding that will permit the manager to operate successfully within the system and even to manipulate it to his own advantage.

As practically all business organizations have functioned for many years, these five principal determining influences on middle managers' behavior have directed managers' interest and effort toward economic objectives. This concentration on economic performance, not only above social considerations but even, as some recently reported instances have revealed, above normal ethical considerations, is for most managers reinforced by almost every significant conditioning factor in their training and experience. Today's middle managers grew up in a culture in which the dominant ethos was suffused by the belief that economic growth was the source of all progress. By the time questions were beginning to be raised about the continuing legitimacy of this theory, most members of this management generation were within the business system and under the influence of the organizational forces described above.

An important conditioning element for managers within this culture was, of course, their educational experience. For a large proportion of the present corps of middle managers, this experience included a business curriculum at either undergraduate or M.B.A. level (a significant number were undergraduate business majors who then continued their concentration in M.B.A. programs). Even in 1980, issues related to corporate social performance have only minimal representation in most business school curricula, and the primacy of economic objectives in all policy formulation and performance evaluation situations is rarely evaluated. It is worth noting that the same relative emphasis is reflected in the content of most executive development programs whether conducted by graduate business schools, by trade and professional organizations, or within corporations.

Perhaps an even more pervasive, if subtler, influence on middle managers is exerted by their perception of society's prevailing standards for measuring personal accomplishment. Although there is a growing disposition among millions of adults to question corporate social behavior as it impacts on the environment, on employees, on customers, on communities, and even on accepted ethical standards, the governing philosophy in our culture is still overwhelmingly materialistic. "Getting ahead" is still generally measured by the acquisition of larger quantities of higher-quality products and services. We are just beginning to confront some of the hard trade-offs among economic and social objectives—as between ample energy supplies and an expanding economy, on one side, and some of the more extreme targets of dedicated environmentalists, on the other. It is at least interesting—possibly of substantial significance—that the initial popular reaction in a number of tough trade-off situations has been to back away from extreme standards of environmental hygiene when confronted by a credible threat of curtailed economic growth.

Value-forming and behavior-determining influences working on middle managers in their prebusiness lives, in their current off-the-job environment, and within their business organizations combine to emphasize economic over social considerations. Obviously, this judgment does not apply to all middle managers. They are not sheltered from the doubts and questions that trouble a growing number outside corporate management ranks. But they are under more pressure, subject to stronger motivation,

177

than outsiders to resist any intellectual or emotional accommodation that might appear to superiors or peers to be a weakening of commitment to traditional corporate objectives.

Middle Managers' Perception of Corporate Social Performance Objectives

In the turbulent business environment of recent years the principal criticisms of corporate social performance naturally have been directed to top management. While middle managers are often confronted by specific local issues—protests by women and minorities over employment and promotion practices, protests by community groups over environmental pollution incidents, probing by communications media into the economic and social effects of production cutbacks or plant closings, union protests over issues of safety and hygiene of working conditions—in the absence of established corporate policies these issues are transmitted rapidly to higher authority for guidance or resolution. Since middle managers are rarely directly involved in the deliberations that lead to policy and program decisions related to corporate social performance, they do not experience the intellectual exercise of carefully exploring benefits and costs that is such a valuable aid in becoming mentally and emotionally comfortable with a new fundamental concept in corporate administration. For most middle managers, internal pressures for technical and economic performance focus their attention on ongoing operations. Except for the probably small minority with a wide-ranging curiosity about the general condition and movement of our society, they are observers of reported events.

178

From the middle managers' viewpoint, corporate social performance policy statements and program decisions usually appear with little advance warning or educational preparation. Suddenly managers are confronted by new performance requirements that not only revise established standards and practices but also threaten to constrain managers' ability to achieve established operating goals, which they view as their primary responsibility.

An instruction to take positive steps to hire women and minorities and to promote those already employed is more than a simple modification in personnel procedures. It raises difficult problems of reactions of existing employees, effects on seniority practices, threats to productivity, and customer attitudes. An instruction to revise procurement practices with the objective of directing more business to minority-owned suppliers is more than a modest revision in the placement of purchase orders. It poses troubling considerations about acquisition costs, quality assurance, delivery schedules, continuity of operations, and even the need to provide special management counsel and financial assistance to marginal suppliers. An instruction to include investment for pollution control in capital budget proposals is more than a procedural stipulation. It raises the probability of reduced return on assets and curtailed appropriations for the support of ongoing or new productive activities. These are not trivial issues for middle managers. They are loaded with economic performance and career implications that cannot fail to be deeply troubling and confusing.

These disturbing effects are likely to be reinforced if, as is usually the case, social performance policies and operating directives are communicated downstream as individual top-management decisions, rather than in the

179

context of a comprehensive reorientation of the total business aimed at coordinating economic and social performance. The piecemeal approach to policy declaration inevitably appears to many subordinate managers as the kind of high-level public relations that invites a skeptical assessment of its operating significance. A comparable fragmented approach to practices in personnel, procurement, investment, and other affected areas also invites a hostile reaction because of the perceived effect on measured economic performance.

Against this background it should not be surprising that middle managers' attitudes toward social performance policies and programs communicated down through the organization from corporate headquarters commonly are in the range from skeptical through indifferent to hostile. At one end of the spectrum, managers assess the announcements as designed for external publics, without significant meaning within the organization. At the other extreme, they see a real threat to their own careers. Skepticism leads to inaction and, at best, to superficial gestures toward compliance in anticipation of weak follow-up through supervisory channels. Fear leads to hostility and a disposition to identify and magnify difficulties in putting instructions into effect.

Another issue may be of even greater substance than the negative attitudes. Some social performance policies and programs call for knowledge and skills that many middle managers lack and know they lack, or expose managers to problems they prefer not to face because they are uncertain about their competence for handling them successfully. A manager who has never supervised an employee group in which minorities constitute a significant element may well wonder whether he will confront problems of communication, motivation, discipline, and productivity. He may anticipate a degree of culture shock to which he will not readily adjust. Regardless of his assessment of his own ability to administer effectively in such a situation, he may have serious concern about difficult relationships within his employee group, particularly if members of the established group sense reverse discrimination.

Culture shock of a different character is likely to be anticipated by middle managers who have no experience in working with women in subordinate or peer management positions. At the least, they sense the introduction of new and uncomfortable relationships and disturbance of familiar behavior patterns. Middle managers who have never represented their companies in confrontations with community or interest group leaders, or with the media, have good reason to doubt their competence in such situations. There is little in their earlier training and work experience on which they can draw for guidance.

The superficially attractive solution to all of these difficulties of attitude, knowledge, and skill is to educate managers to understand and handle their new duties and responsibilities. Carefully planned educational programs, designed with a real grasp of managers' genuine concerns as well as their cultural blocks, will help. In particular, they will add to managers' understanding of social changes and their perception of operating problems in carrying out specific social performance programs. But education alone is not likely to have any material effect in converting negative into positive attitudes. Indifferent or destructive attitudes reflect a conflict between managers' perception of the requirements for effective implementation of social performance policies and programs, and their perception of the requirements for advancing their own careers. Until these perceptions are reconciled, any educational effort will be handicapped by the absence of strong motivation among participating managers and of clear reinforcement through the formal reward-penalty system. As every professional educator knows, strong motivation to learn and clear reinforcement of lessons learned through respected rewards and penalties are essential for successful learning and for constructive behavior.

With respect to the educational program itself, it should also be observed that the required educational materials are not immediately available in "off-the-intellectual-shelf" inventories. The introduction of social performance considerations into business organizations is a genuine innovation. It creates new management problems of substantial complexity in both analysis and action. Developing the required managerial knowledge and skills will generate a need for new educational materials. For example, there is currently available only a small stock of cases that report actual experiences of business organizations in attempting to implement social performance policies and programs. No more than a beginning has been made toward defining either the information requirements or the analytical techniques involved in forecasting trends in public expectations and demands for corporate social performance. Little is known about how to relate projected trends to the task of defining practical opportunities for and limitations on responses by individual companies. New accounting concepts and systems must be developed to facilitate the extension of cost-benefit analysis to social as well as economic considerations. In short, progress in identifying and providing needed materials for the educational experience must be supported by appropriate motivational and operating machinery.

Redesigning the Total Management System

What is required is comprehensive redesign of the total management system to reflect the incorporation of new social objectives along with traditional economic objectives. The existing structure of specific management objectives, performance measurement, and rewards and penalties was designed to facilitate and motivate the accomplishment of economic goals. Until this structure is appropriately modified, policy pronouncements and program determinations at the senior administrative level will not be fully credible or respected at lower organizational levels. Where attainment of social performance goals is perceived as interfering with the attainment of economic performance goals, the former will be sacrificed to the latter to the extent necessary to assure satisfactory economic performance. In these circumstances, skepticism about senior management's sincerity and resolve will fester and educational programs will not be effective.

The first step in adapting the corporate management system to put social objectives on a par with economic objectives is clear communication by the chief executive officer of the meaning of the new corporate philosophy and the rationale for adopting it. The statement should note that what is projected is not an erosion of the organization's economic mission, but instead is an accommodation to the facts of life in contemporary society, an accommodation that will be mandated by the society if voluntary initiatives are not taken by business. The communication should point out that in many areas of social concern with business behavior there are opportunities for corporate actions that will be economically advantageous to organizations whose managers have the imagination and will to act vigorously ahead of competitors. In other areas where action by a single company may not be feasible for competitive reasons, there may be advantageous opportunities to influence the standards and procedures of public regulation.

This is not a simple message for the chief executive officer to articulate or for middle managers to understand and accept. Understanding and acceptance can be encouraged and assisted by a variety of supporting measures. The unqualified endorsement of the new administrative philosophy by the board of directors must be visible to all managers. This endorsement will be strengthened if the composition, structure, and work of the board reflect a commitment to broader participation in membership by qualified persons who are knowledgeable about societal concerns and who will closely scrutinize management performance in these areas. Understanding and acceptance can be further assisted by small-group meetings in which senior line and staff officers take the lead in discussing the rationale for the changed view of the mission of the business and in articulating their unqualified commitment to it.

This top-down communications process is no more than a stage set, however. Carefully and thoroughly programmed and conducted, it will facilitate the introduction of modifications in the decision-making and decision-implementing process through which the organization functions. Unless followed up by appropriate changes in that process, its effect is more likely to be negative than positive. It could have the effect of increasing middle managers' skepticism about top management's commitment to the announced new view of the social performance of the business.

Most middle managers will not accept social performance as a concept with real operating significance until they see it incorporated in specific terms in their assigned duties and responsibilities, until specific time-phased social performance objectives are built into their operating budgets, until their accomplishment of these objectives is systematically measured just as their accomplishment of budgeted economic targets is measured, and until each manager's measured social performance is visibly brought within the scope of the reward-penalty system. What all this involves is no less than a major transformation in fundamental corporate administration.

This transformation will be both easier to accomplish in some ways and more difficult in others than was the initial institution of the now-familiar administrative system that defines economic performance objectives for operating units, determines responsibility for achieving them, measures results, and motivates appropriate managerial behavior. It will be easier to accomplish because it utilizes existing performance concepts and existing control systems. It will be more difficult to accomplish because the initial steps to define specific social performance objectives will immediately and dramatically reveal the complex network of relationships among economic and social performance objectives, their competitive claims on limited corporate resources, and the need to develop a vocabulary and an arithmetic for describing and evaluating economic and social costs and benefits within an integrated decision system. As in the experience with economic performance control systems, the specification of objectives and related resource requirements will promptly illuminate conflicting claims and compel managers to think about and agree on priorities. These factors then will have to be worked through trade-offs among social performance programs, and also through trade-offs between economic and social objectives.

In spite of these difficulties there should be no doubt that middle managers' understanding, acceptance, and implementation of social performance policies and programs—whatever their content as determined by senior management—are absolutely dependent on full and specific incorporation of the policies and programs within the administrative system of the business. Anything short of such a comprehensive approach will weaken the credibility of the corporate posture among the managers whose commitment is essential for converting policy into practice.

Special Management Training Needs

One additional requirement must be satisfied to assure implementation of social performance policies and programs at a level of operating effectiveness and efficiency comparable to that achieved for economic performance in successful companies. Some of the administrative tasks associated with social performance programs raise problems that are outside the education and experience of most managers. Dealing with these issues calls for skills that few operating executives have developed through prior training and practice, or can work up on their own initiative. They need training, just as do operating managers in corporations that install formal long-range planning systems.

The most urgent training needs are in two areas. The first is managing nondiscriminatory personnel policies and practices in factory, office, and management ranks. The second is managing relationships with external publics and with communications media. In both areas the critical issue is not what to do, but how to do it. What to do is easily defined. The difficulty here, as noted above, is credibility, and the tactics that will strengthen credibility are readily applied by determined, sophisticated senior management. How to do it is another matter altogether, one in which imaginative training programs in a few companies are already making valuable contributions.

In personnel administration, the central problem can be described as one of cultural adjustment, although the term should not be interpreted as dismissing substantive issues in such sensitive areas as seniority prerogatives and perceived reverse discrimination. Friction and resistance in these areas are not trivial matters, of course, but external social pressures, as well as governmental actions, are working to assist corporate managers to develop formulas of accommodation that will be acceptable to conflicting interests. On the whole, there is more noise than substance here, and even the noise will diminish in an expanding economy.

The cultural adjustment is less spectacular but more difficult to handle. Most middle managers are not accustomed to and are not at ease with an organizational environment in which many subordinate, peer, and superior management positions are occupied by members of minority groups and women. They anticipate encountering and in reality they do encounter unfamiliar behavior and terms of interpersonal relationships. The problems are not significantly different from those met by American managers who are posted to a foreign country where their associates are nationals, and who are not adequately prepared in language, customs, traditions, attitudes—all that goes to make up a unique culture.

As experience in multinationals suggests, left to their own resources most managers ultimately learn how to make the essential cultural adjustments, although often painfully and slowly. Some cannot come to terms with the alien environment (or their families fail the test) and have to be withdrawn. Carefully planned training programs can build the understanding and develop the skills required for a faster and easier adjustment. As a useful side effect, such programs may also facilitate early identification of those who cannot be helped to function effectively outside their national culture. Comparable training programs can help managers accustomed to the behavior of white male management groups to develop the skills required for working with minority and female associates. The experience of a few organizations suggests that "real-life" cases and role-playing encounters are particularly valuable in challenging stereotyped traditional attitudes and encouraging the recognition and application of relevant administrative and interpersonal skills. The time and money costs of a thorough training program will be more than compensated by its contribution to alleviating the damaging effects of culture shock and speeding the adjustment process.

Training needs are both more obvious and considerably simpler in the area of relationships with external publics and communications media. For most middle managers this is a radical enlargement of traditional job responsibilities. They have little preparation in training or experience for dealing with community or special interest groups in adversary situations, such as those connected with environmental contamination, factory hygiene, and personnel practices. With rare exceptions, they have had no exposure to media representatives, no occasion to formulate policy positions under pressure and articulate them clearly and forcefully to reporters and before television cameras. Yet with growing frequency middle managers responsible for plant, geographic, or product operations find themselves in positions where they must speak for their organizations and where what they say and how they say it can have a critical effect, positive or negative, on public attitudes and even on governmental decisions.

They need help, and fortunately they know they need help. So, for that matter, do senior corporate officers, who are also frequently called upon to speak for their organizations in adversary face-to-face situations and on television. A well-designed training program can build the kind of understanding of constituency group attitudes and tactics and of the politics of media relations that is essential for developing reasonable and constructive corporate positions that effectively accommodate public and corporate interests. It can also improve managers' communications skills and strengthen their confidence in their ability to address public audiences directly and through print and electronic media. As a not inconsequential by-product, it can also bring to the attention of senior officers individuals who are unusually effective in such situations, an ability that is likely to be given increasing attention in future promotion decisions.

NOTE: Some of the material in this chapter appeared in different form in the author's paper "Governance Issues within the Corporate Management Structure," in *Running the American Corporation*, edited by William R. Dill (Englewood Cliffs, N.J.: Prentice-Hall, 1978).

9

Relations with Nonmanagement Employees

A COMMITMENT to place social performance objectives on a par with economic objectives will create or exacerbate a variety of difficulties in a company's relations with its nonmanagement employees. In one form or another, problems are likely to be encountered with all groups of employees: union and nonunion, factory and office, male and female, white and black, young and old, skilled and unskilled. Some of the pressures will also affect the behavior and attitudes of first- and second-line supervisors, partly because they share many of the concerns of nonmanagement employees and partly because they experience the direct impact of their subordinates' disaffections.

Specific Problem Areas

If the problems can be identified in advance, appropriate policies, programs, and procedures can be planned

190

to avert or ameliorate most of the difficulties. Anticipating explosive, abrasive, or sensitive issues is not an overwhelmingly difficult task. It requires knowledge and skills, however, that many managers have only limited experience in developing and applying. The knowledge and skill requirements extend beyond those normally required in the traditional personnel administration function. In some high-pressure circumstances managers must absorb the traumatic discovery of fiercely protective parochial cultures within the American society.

The nature and incidence of specific problems and the difficulty of coping with them will be largely determined by one or more of the following social and political factors in an organization's internal environment:

1. *The extent to which the new policies, programs, and procedures are perceived by employees to change or modify established rules and practices.* It makes little difference whether the existing order is the result of formal, even contractual, commitments, or is simply a set of accepted customs reinforced by years of consistent management and employee behavior. It also matters little whether the innovations intrude on central elements in the work environment, or would be evaluated as peripheral or even trivial by any uninvolved observer. The real issue is the necessity to revise familiar routines with which most employees feel comfortable and therefore secure.

2. *The extent to which the new policies, programs, and procedures are perceived as removing, curtailing, or threatening specific existing economic and social rights and privileges of employees.* If some of these rights and privileges are not the product of unilateral management commitment, but are incorporated in a union contract, the introduction of change is cast into a rigid legal framework. But the management issues may be almost as sticky in the absence of contractual obligations, or even in the absence of a bargaining relationship. Here the issue is more than interference with familiar routines. It is deprivation (real or perceived) of special benefits.

3. *The extent to which the organization has a history of*

stable growth free from short-term fluctuations in scale of operations. The critical arena is not the corporation as a whole. Rather, it is the individual work unit (plant, department, sales territory, office center) where employees perceive themselves as participants in a common economic and social environment, sharing common loyalties and concerns, and enclosed within a common job and career security structure. The issue here is whether the real or perceived adjustments are accepted as capable of being absorbed within the familiar process of growth without threatening the benefits enjoyed by existing employees, or the reverse. If, for example, job and career opportunities for previously disadvantaged minorities can be created, or are viewed as able to be created, only by constraining or denying comparable opportunities for existing employees, management faces a difficult task.

4. *The extent to which the affected employee group is diversified in ethnic, racial, cultural, sex, and age composition.* In general, pluralistic diversified groups are likely to be less hostile and resistant than homogeneous groups to changes in the real or perceived work environment. A diversified employee population lacks a uniform set of values and attitudes. Informal leadership roles are exercised by a number of individuals. Some of these leaders may even see in the innovation opportunities for personal political advantage in supporting management interests against those of other employee leaders.

5. *The extent to which management possesses credibility and trust, its administrative policies and practices are regarded as generally fair and reasonable, and open communication channels are maintained with a history of active use by managers and employees.* Employees' belief that they work for an organization in which management is generally frank and truthful can be a critical factor in reducing unreasoning opposition to any of the real or perceived changes that are involved in bringing social objectives to rough equality with economic objectives.

It is an awkward but inescapable fact that these factors, which are so influential in determining the complexity of the management task in introducing or advancing social

192

performance considerations, must be accepted as givens in any problem situation. An organization's condition in each of these regards reflects the totality of its prior history and cannot be significantly modified in the short term. Whatever policies and programs management may decide to undertake must therefore be formulated in the context of these constraints.

Critical Considerations for Management

Employees' concern with a corporation's social performance policies and programs—and therefore their attitudes and actions—will not be uniform with respect to all social performance areas. Subject as they are to many of the same forces and influences that impact on management, their natural interest is the personal pay-off of each corporate move. The pay-off may be clearly and accurately assessed, or it may be misjudged. It may be assessed to be advantageous or threatening. Its significance may be assessed as massive or trivial. And in the end it may be supported, accepted, or vehemently opposed and even sabotaged.

Discrete employee categories within a total employee population inevitably are affected in different ways and degrees by individual corporate social performance policies and programs. There is a high probability, therefore, of a mixed response to most specific management initiatives. Probably the only areas of social performance action where at least some nonmanagement employees may not be sensitive to possible favorable or adverse impacts are those involving a company's relations with its customers, in such matters as product quality, terms of sale, guarantees, service, and advertising and other commercial communications.

193

The attitudes of employees are also subject to the influence of external organizations and interest groups, including unions, community organizations, religious institutions, and organizations promoting the special interests of racial, ethnic, sex, and age groups. Beyond this, of course, they share with all of us a dependence on news and opinion supplied by the communications media.

Several considerations of critical importance in formulating corporate social performance strategy are suggested by this complex set of conditions. In analyzing these considerations, management must deal with the opportunities and constraints created by the organization's social and political system: (1) the interplay of special interest groups with their array of parallel, divergent, and competing objectives; (2) real or perceived threats to established (by contract, policy, or custom) employee rights and privileges; (3) real or perceived conflicts among broadly supported societal goals, organizational goals, and the differentiated goals of discrete employee groups (racial, ethnic, sex, age, skill, seniority); and (4) the structure and dynamics of the formal and informal political systems through which employees' attitudes are mobilized and articulated and their needs serviced.

The familiar tools of economic analysis offer little help in unraveling these social and political complexities. Efforts to apply a cost-benefit calculus, for example, usually run afoul of differences among groups in the incidence of specific costs and benefits. Moreover, the influences of external groups on employees' values and attitudes are difficult to assess and impossible to censor or control.

In the context of all these diverse elements, the first consideration in developing a management strategy for implementing social performance objectives, policies, and programs is identification of specific positive, neutral, and negative interests within the employee population. These form the basis for potential support for and opposition to individual social performance policies and programs. These positive and negative nuclei will not be identical for all social performance issues. Supportive and opposed constituencies will be uniquely defined for each issue. Employees will appraise the probability and intensity of beneficial, neutral, or adverse impacts on their present and future rights and privileges.

The probability and intensity of perceived effects are themselves under the influence of dynamic social and political conditions within and outside the organization. Employees are not unaware of the pressure on management to adapt corporate conduct to changing social expectations for the role and behavior of business organizations. Employees are themselves part of the influencing society and share its values.

These dualities often contribute to unnecessary confusion in management thinking about employee relations in this area. Equally with many senior managers, employees are capable of holding favorable attitudes toward improved environmental hygiene as a generally desirable social objective, while opposing a specific government mandate to invest in pollution control equipment at their own semiobsolete plant, particularly if management makes a persuasive economic case for closing the facility rather than adding to nonproductive costs. Like some managers, some employees may favor equal employment and career opportunities for disadvantaged groups as a general social goal, while resisting the application of such a policy when they fear its infringement on their own status and prospects for advancement. In short, these are not novel attitudes. They do not present unfamiliar problems to a chief executive officer who has observed similar dualities operating within management ranks—and possibly within his own mind.

195

On the positive side, the disparity of employee interests related to almost every significant corporate social performance objective and policy also represents an opportunity to mobilize useful support for any specific program. It is hard to imagine a single example of changing corporate social behavior where management could identify a hostile attitude endorsed by substantially all employees. It is, of course, possible to cite examples of near-unanimous positive endorsement—generally characterized by visible benefits for employees unaccompanied by economic or social costs borne by them. Even here, however, a thorough skeptic might anticipate pockets of dissent in favor of trading social investment for direct increases in wages and other benefits.

Identification of employee groups that are likely to support or oppose a specific social performance policy or program provides a foundation for information and action strategies. To the extent that certain employee groups favor a policy or program, they can be a resource in neutralizing or countering other employee groups who conclude that their special interest is best served by active opposition. Such support can be valuable both within the organization and in external community relationships.

Employee support may also be a valuable resource when management's analysis of costs and benefits leads to a decision not to comply with pressures targeted on a company by external activists (including, in extreme situations, government regulatory agencies). The uneconomic demands of zealots for a cause can be countered much more effectively when management's refusal to comply is publicly endorsed by employee groups. The power of such an alliance has been documented in a number of environmental confrontations.

In evaluating the general feasibility of broadening the

base of support for both positive and negative decisions on social performance issues, management must understand the critical importance of its credibility with its employees. If management's prior behavior has encouraged skepticism or distrust, there is no possibility for establishing instant credibility, even when the specific issue clearly identifies a common interest in the course management proposes to follow.

A second consideration is therefore management's ability to communicate to its employees a credible social performance posture, and to articulate that posture in specific social performance policies and programs. Credibility among employees is essential when management undertakes to state what it intends to do, why it intends to do it, how it intends to do it, and what the anticipated results are going to be. Without such credibility, all that can be reasonably anticipated in response to any proposal is a spreading sense of uncertainty and insecurity.

The effects of uncertainty and insecurity among employees are well known in organizational experience. Rumors of flamboyant character flow through informal communication channels. Resistance to any announced policy or program is almost automatic. Attention is focused on real and imagined negative effects of proposals, while positive and constructive results are ignored or denied. Once into this morass, recovery may be almost impossible.

Two conditions are required to assure the desired degree of employee trust and confidence in management's social performance commitments. The first is a history of frank communications from management to employees, supported by a record of fulfilled commitments. The second is clear articulation of objectives, reasons, methods, and anticipated results, including effects on existing employee rights and privileges. Both elements are essential.

In the absence of the first, the second cannot escape a skeptical response.

A management with a poor internal communications and performance history is likely to face serious difficulties in winning any significant support among its employees when it announces a new social performance policy or program, even if the innovation promises specific benefits for employees. Such an organization is the captive of its own history, and management must reckon with this unpleasant reality in its social performance planning.

This is only part of the story, of course. Management has a similar communications problem (which should also be read as "opportunity") when it decides *not* to respond to a particular pressure for changed social behavior emanating from an outside interest group. It needs to describe and explain its decision to its employees, and to indicate what results, positive or negative, should be anticipated that relate to the interests of both the company and its employees. The reception these messages will receive obviously will also depend on the credibility base established by management's earlier communications and performance record.

Finally, no sophisticated manager will be unaware that effective communication is a two-way flow. It is important for employees to know what management intends to do by way of improving its social performance, and why, and what the effects are likely to be for employees. It is equally important for management to be familiar with social performance concerns of its employees, how these concerns are shared or disputed among employee groups, and what priorities among their various economic and social concerns exist in the thinking of employee groups.

Still a third consideration deserves management attention. This is the possibility of linking external social interests with the interests of internal employee groups. The opportunities for mobilizing constructive influences here run in both directions. Some societal pressures for changes in corporate social performance may be channeled to act on employee groups in a way that will transform their incipient hostility and resistance into active support or, minimally, into passive acceptance of management's commitment to new policies and programs. The area of equitable employment and career practices offers many examples of successful use of this strategy.

Alternatively, when management is under pressure to modify operations in ways that are severely disadvantageous to a company's economic performance and, equally, to employees' job security, employees' defense of their interests can be coordinated with management's opposition in a common defense strategy. Such a strategy has been successful in situations where firms have been subjected to extreme environmental or product performance pressures that ignore severe unbalances of costs and benefits.

Critical Considerations for Employees

The full implications of the array of problems and opportunities in employee relations in the socially responsive corporation cannot be grasped by looking only at the management side of the relationship. The pressures on management for changed social behavior also impact on employees, who are themselves part of the society that is generating the pressures. Even when motivated to protect their own perceived rights and privileges against substantive threats, employees also share in evolving social values. As consumers and citizens, they want improvements in environmental hygiene, in safer products, in removal of inequitable obstructions to employment and career opportunities, in elimination of hazardous working conditions. As taxpayers, they want these benefits without charge or at relatively low cost, preferably with that cost borne by others. Rationally, they appreciate the nonexistence of the free lunch. Emotionally, they want that lunch. Existentially, they slowly and painfully discover, as managers do, the hard rule that the items on the lunch menu have to be evaluated one by one, with whatever crude cost-benefit criteria may be available.

Employees' first consideration in making this evaluation is their perception of the probable direct impact of a specific social performance policy or program on their existing and anticipated rights, privileges, opportunities, and other benefits. A number of influences affect this perception. In most circumstances the most powerful influence is the historically determined set of economic and social values which for any individual are the product of a network of family, community, religious, and educational concepts, tempered by personal experiences in applying these values.

These core values are powerful and trusted guides in familiar situations. They are less powerful in situations that contain novel elements. Here most people are likely to sense the inadequacy of prior guides to conduct. In their insecurity and doubt they are disposed to open their reason and emotions to the influence of other sources of information that command a significant degree of credibility. These sources include friends, fellow workers, news media, unions, religious institutions and individual religious leaders, political parties and individual political leaders, and formal and informal community groups. Depending on employees' experience, management may or may not be a trusted source of information. This influence is subject to the significant qualification that what constitutes "management" may in specific situations lie anywhere along the range from the chief executive officer to a first-level supervisor.

The messages these influences transmit in any novel and pressureful situation cannot fail to exert a strong influence over employees' perception of the probable effect of a specific change on existing and future benefits. The greater the innovation (it matters little whether in reality or perception), the more vivid is likely to be employees' sense of uncertainty, insecurity, even fear, and the more open their minds to persuasion about the meaning of the change to them as individuals. It is precisely in this environment that the strongest attitudes and most vigorous actions are formulated.

An individual employee may have a set of core values that are generally favorable toward the concept of equal employment opportunity and promotion based on merit. He can be jolted into a negative attitude toward the initiation of such a policy in his plant or office, however, if any credible source warns that the probable outcome is invasion of his seniority status, his promotion potential, or his work prerogatives. As cynics predicted and idealists were shocked to discover, large numbers of whites in Northern communities who criticized the slow pace of integration in Southern schools in the 1960s and supported government action to compel compliance with legislation and court orders were induced by local community pressures to change their views radically in the 1970s when integration came to their own schools and their own children.

Management's understanding of the sensitive and volatile character of this interplay of influences among plant and office employees can be an important factor in successful implementation of corporate social performance policies and programs. From such understanding comes recognition of opportunities for and constraints on its own ability to play a constructive role in influencing employees' attitudes and actions. Management must recognize, however, that the weight of its positive influence relative to that of other attitude-forming influences is substantially determined by the credibility it has earned by its prior behavior. This is the heart of the case for assigning employee relations strategies an important place in long-range planning for corporate social performance.

A second consideration for employees is the extent to which they perceive any announced change in corporate social performance as inevitable. The choice among reactions along the range from support, acceptance, and accommodation to resistance, all-out opposition, and even the desperate negativism of sabotage is a judgment affected by both long-held and newly accepted values. It is also influenced by anticipation of the nature and timing of the probable outcome of the announced change. This assessment process resembles the comparable assessment made by many middle-level managers who see their status and career prospects as likely to be affected by their organization's new social performance policies and programs and are trying to sort out the relevant factors for an appropriate personal response.

Employees' judgments about the inevitability of a new corporate social policy or procedure are shaped both by their perception of developments in the external environment and by the operational vigor applied by management in carrying out the change within the organization. External developments include the obvious legislative and regulatory actions. They also encompass positions publicly articulated by nongovernmental institutions and opinion leaders, and the statements and activities of interest groups in local communities. Internal developments generally center on management's visible creation of organizational structures and administrative machinery for implementing its announced policies, supported by its perceived commitment to make the system work to achieve described results. As every manufacturing manager and factory worker knows, there is all the difference in the world between promoting safety in plant operations through exhortations and wall posters, and instituting a safety program that invests in protective devices for dangerous equipment, applies sanctions to supervisors who fail to insist on adherence to prescribed safety practices, and trains employees in risk-avoiding work procedures and methods. The former is an open invitation to skepticism; the latter commands respect and compliance, even when the requirements are tedious or uncomfortable.

An important factor in management strategy therefore is its ability to set its social performance commitments within a framework that clearly communicates the message of inevitability. Mandated compliance with applicable law, regulatory directive, or judicial finding is the strongest and clearest platform for management policy. It is also, however, of the least significance and interest for corporate strategy formulation. Much more important and difficult is the establishment of a high degree of perceived inevitability for social performance commitments in the absence of external mandates. Equally important, and often even more difficult, is the establishment of a comparable perception of inevitability for a decision against a social performance commitment. Both require detailed and persuasive presentation of the reasons for the decision, its associated economic and social costs and benefits, and the organizational and operational arrangements for its implementation.

A third consideration in employees' evaluation of some corporate social performance policies and programs is their perception of the presence of a margin of accommodation that will facilitate or ease in the incidence of any change. This perception is particularly significant in their assessment of an innovation that threatens to intrude on established practices. The critical factor in their judgment of the margin of accommodation in any specific situation is therefore the extent to which they believe change will be substantially absorbed through growth, attrition, or some other "cushion," with minimum disturbance of existing conditions. A management decision to open new employment and career opportunities for women and minorities, for example, is perceived in different perspectives by employees who are accustomed to sustained growth, by employees accustomed to stability without significant growth, by employees in severely unstable activities who have experienced alternating hiring and lay-off, and by employees in contracting organizations. Perceptions of the margin of accommodation are also affected by the time scale of change and by the presence or absence of provisions for protecting all or most employees from possible adverse effects of change.

Management's ability to capitalize on favorable aspects of the margin-of-accommodation consideration is obviously limited by external product and market conditions over which it has, at best, only limited control. To the extent that these conditions are favorable, of course, they should be incorporated in planning for the nature, scope, and timing of changes in social performance that are likely to be perceived by employees as affecting their interests. With respect to internal conditions, however, sensitive and imaginative management can take significant steps to formulate and administer the introduction of change in ways that minimize hostile reaction by providing protective buffers for sensitive employee interests. Where these possibilities exist or can be created, it is clearly advantageous to use them.

There is neither sophistry nor hypocrisy in such a strategy. The preservation of benefits for existing employees is a legitimate element in assessing the gross benefits associated with corporate social performance. Equally, any increase in economic or social costs borne by existing employees is a legitimate element in assessing the total costs associated with corporate performance.

Relations with Unions and Their Officers

Social performance strategy issues involving relations with unions, particularly with their national and local leaders, present a special case within the general set of issues involving relations with plant and office employees. The unique characteristics of the union situation deserve identification as a basis for strategy formulation. It is especially important to recognize that the union relationship should not be viewed as an inevitable obstacle to the accomplishment of a company's social performance objectives. Some of its characteristics create opportunities to build cooperation and support for management policies and programs. On occasion, this support may also be enlisted for management decisions to resist certain pressures from external interest groups, such as environmentalists, whose proposals disregard substantial economic and social costs associated with the social benefits they are energetically promoting.

It has become clear in recent years that union organizations and their leaders are very much involved with the same changing societal expectations for business behavior that have so sharply challenged corporate management. As power structures that can influence both the external environment in which they function and the internal environment in which they represent and bargain for their members' interests, they are widely viewed as responsible for how they use their power. Abuse of their power, or failure to use it in a manner that contributes to approved social goals, invites public criticism, censure, mandates, and sanctions in a pattern that resembles the treatment of unsatisfactory performers among business organizations.

Public assessment of the behavior of union institutions along these lines seems likely to increase in the future, again parallel to the prospects for business institutions. A growing number of union leaders are indicating their sensitivity to this development and acknowledging, often as reluctantly as some corporate leaders, the need to administer their responsibilities in the broader public context as well as in relation to their members' economic and social concerns.

How unions and their officers handle this responsibility is affected, of course, by the fact that unions are political institutions and their officers are politicians in a way that is distinctly different from business organizations and their executives. The ultimate power in business organizations is at the top; in unions it is at the bottom. Further, as a result of rather intense and generally successful public and membership pressures in recent years to democratize the political process within unions, that ultimate power is asserting itself. Recognition of this development influences union officers' attitudes and behavior in specific corporate social performance situations.

Sophisticated managers know the importance of analyzing union strategies and tactics in relation to their political as well as their economic contexts in contract negotiations and in ongoing administration of approved contracts. Such managers will readily grasp, and others will need to discover, the positive and negative potentials of the political structure and dynamism of unions. This can be a significant factor in formulating corporate social performance policies and programs, and in implementing decisions on what to do and how to do it. It also can affect decisions on what to resist doing and how to make that resistance effective.

Considerations that grow out of the internal politics of union organizations relate in a variety of ways, often unique to each local facility, to the positions that union leaders will publicly adopt and vigorously implement with respect to pollution, product safety, safety and hygiene of work place and process, fair employment, intracompany due process, and other matters on the corporate social performance menu. In some of these areas perceived union interests and politically feasible public postures may lead to a decision to oppose social performance policies and programs favored by management. But there will be numerous situations in which economic interests and political feasibility (on occasion even political necessity) will lead to either, at best, union endorsement and active support of the management commitment or, at worst, neutrality. Union support can be particularly useful in dealing with legislative and regulatory agencies when management is opposing specific mandated actions that will impose substantial economic or social costs on an industry, a company, or a facility. This is a resource that should not be overlooked.

Managers experienced in collective bargaining understand the gaps often encountered between the private views of individual union leaders on appropriate or necessary social performance policies and the views popular among their rank-and-file membership. Because of the political structure of unions—especially in those unions in which democratic procedures are practiced and in which insurgencies are a real threat to leadership—it is not easy and often may not be prudent for a union officer to adopt or recommend a position that many members will perceive as contrary to their interests. An additional complexity is that discriminatory personnel practices have long existed in a number of industries, by informal management-labor agreement or indirect incorporation in formal contracts. In these situations more than an intrusion on folkways is at stake, although even this intrusion is a serious administrative problem.

Another aspect of the issue that deserves management consideration is the intensifying pressure on national union leaders to accept social responsibilities similar to those proposed for business leaders. The traditional social contract for business was also, by indirection, a social contract for unions. The practical reality of this association is documented by the commitment to the capitalistic enterprise system by American union leaders and an overwhelming majority of rank-and-file members, and the absence of the kind of radical socialist-oriented unionism so prevalent in Western Europe.

It is apparent that although the brightest spotlight continues to shine on business responses to social needs and expectations, union attitudes will engage increasing public attention. This is particularly likely to occur if a substantial body of public opinion concludes that obduracy on the union side constrains progress toward widely supported social improvement. This book argues that opposition by corporate leaders to strongly supported social demands for changed corporate behavior is likely to lead to an extension in the breadth and depth of governmental regulation of business, with the enlarged regulation largely designed by ill-informed but zealous reformers. An equally strong case can be made for the proposition that union opposition to social demands for changed behavior is likely to lead to comparable restriction of union independence. It is not probable that our society will accept one code of conduct for corporations and another for unions. In the last analysis, therefore, corporations and unions have a preponderance of mutual, rather than adversary, interests.

Union leaders cannot escape the same hard lessons that business leaders have been confronting. A responsibility of leadership, in some critical situations, is to educate and motivate followers. Those union leaders who see this issue clearly, and some do already, have a powerful reason to use their credibility with their membership to join farseeing management in taking necessary actions to preserve an enterprise system in which they and their members have as vital a stake as managers (and the owners by whom they are employed).

Corporate leaders should be intensely interested in the development of union thinking in this area. Since many corporate social performance policies and programs—not limited to those related to personnel administration—can be implemented more quickly and effectively with the cooperation of union leadership than against its overt or covert opposition, corporate management should search for ways to engage that cooperation. Together, corporate managers and union leaders can help to preserve a set of common institutions by reasoned accommodation to a changing society.

10

Relations with Publics

THE corporation that undertakes to put social objectives on a par with economic objectives must redesign both its traditional public relations function and the traditional role of its chief public relations officer. These changes are essential for several reasons.

Such a company, first, has an enlarged requirement to describe and interpret for senior operating management current and projected developments and attitudes among the many publics with which the organization has relationships: shareholders, employees, customers, suppliers, distributors, local communities, government officials, and a variety of special interest groups (women, minorities, the old, the young, environmentalists, consumers, etc.). Serving this requirement demands a comprehensive and sophisticated understanding of social activities and trends together with an imaginative grasp of their implications for business in general and for the individual company in particular.

Second, there is a new requirement to evaluate for operating management the social implications of proposed corporate policies and programs, which usually are appraised solely in the context of economic objectives. This requirement will draw not only on the public relations officer's sensitive perception of how the corporation's normal operations may be viewed by special interest groups, including those not obviously affected by specific business practices. It will also tap his ability to communicate his perceptions persuasively to senior managers.

Third, there is an important opportunity for the public relations officer to propose for senior management consideration policies and programs whose justification originates in the area of social, rather than economic, performance. This opportunity to participate actively in the policy formulation process will require that the public relations officer have both the degree of credibility among senior managers necessary for serious evaluation of proposals initiated outside their accustomed decision range, and the ability to apply the cost-benefit calculus in areas where it has seldom been used.

Finally, there is a requirement for planning and executing communications programs directed to various publics on a scale and at a level of sophistication which few organizations have previously attempted. This requirement includes counseling and assisting corporate officers and managers who participate in communications programs, an assignment for which most managers are ill prepared. Their perceptiveness and skill are likely to be critical to the success of the total communication effort.

The Traditional Public Relations Function

The magnitude of the changes involved in meeting these requirements is dramatically exposed when these requirements are evaluated in the context of the traditional corporate public relations function. That function generally is concerned with preparing and transmitting two classes of communications to various publics. The first category, large in volume and occasionally technical in content, is product publicity. This primarily involves preparing news stories about company products and services and placing the stories in media appropriate for transmitting the information to selected target publics. Product publicity is part of the communications component in a comprehensive marketing program.

The second category, growing in scale in recent years, is corporate publicity—the preparation and communication of information about a company's policies, actions, people, or other aspects of its operations to one or more external publics. Corporate publicity is often described as "image building," a term of invidious connotation for an activity that may be both economically valuable and morally respectable. On some occasions corporate publicity is an offensive communications strategy, designed to transmit information favorable to the sponsoring organization. At other times it is a defensive strategy, aimed at portraying unfavorable information in a favorable manner. Sometimes, of course, the strategic objective may be to minimize media reporting of information about a company in situations in which management's goal is "the less said the better, and nothing said is best of all."

In both aspects of the traditional public relations function the director of the activity serves in what is essentially a dependent or passive role in relation to decisions on corporate policies and programs. Here, he is told in effect, is a new or improved company product, process, or service: prepare and place the stories that will bring the news to the attention of the appropriate public in a manner that will arouse maximum awareness and interest.

Or, here is a new corporate policy or action that should be publicized: prepare and place the story in the appropriate media.

In all situations of this general character, the decision that creates the potential news is made by operating managers, usually without advance consultation with the public relations director. The social implications of the decision, if any, are not usually part of the standard decision process, nor do issues at the company's interface with any of its publics ordinarily become significant considerations in the initial phase of policy formulation. One of the more flagrant examples of this process was provided by the revelation that the decision to try to defuse Ralph Nader's first critical attack on the safety of a General Motors product by finding a vulnerable point in Nader's life and habits was made by a corporate lawyer without consulting the public relations director. The adverse publicity aroused by this ill-considered action was embarrassing to management and caused considerable erosion of the favorable public image that the corporation had been working to create over many years. Similar examples, equally painful to the affected managements although less dramatic on the national business scene, could be cited from the experiences of other firms.

This limited and passive traditional public relations function must be reformulated in an active and creative mode, admitted to participation in the general policy-making process, and staffed with professional talent of a kind and quality consistent with its radically changed responsibilities. This is no trivial requirement. It is not a criticism of a large proportion of those who presently direct the corporate public relations function to observe that they are not equipped by education, experience, or organizational status to fulfill the requirement in all its dimensions. The professional background of most public relations practitioners has been in some aspect of journalism, and properly so in relation to the traditional scope and duties of the function. Journalistic skills of a high order will continue to be an essential resource for the manager of the public relations function in the socially responsive corporation. To these technical skills, however, must be joined an understanding of the phenomena and processes of social change, the complex relationships between economic and social performance, and, within the corporate structure, the management decision system and its component management information system.

Beyond these skill and knowledge requirements, tomorrow's effective corporate public relations director will be an individual who by preparation and performance holds the confidence of senior operating managers, of whom few presently understand the importance of the enlarged public relations function and even fewer perceive and respect its fundamental role in coordinating social with economic objectives.

Early Warnings: Perceptions and Evaluations

In reformulating the scope and content of the public relations function, the starting point must be an effort to give specific operational meaning to the term "social objectives." Exactly what is it that a corporation's management is advised to do by the general recommendation to place "social objectives on a par with economic objectives"? About economic objectives there is no question. However measured and however influenced by a particular management's values related to such considerations as risk, stability, and continuity, the basic content of the phrase in all corporations is always focused on profitable growth with explicit quantitative and qualitative characteristics. For an individual company, environmental conditions that are the source of opportunities and threats, and internal resources that define feasibility limits for operations, combine to determine growth and profit potential. While accomplishing economic objectives in the context of competitive dynamics is a difficult assignment, the goals are clear enough. Managers' views may differ about the scale and timing of economic achievement, but not about the meaning of what they are trying to accomplish.

To most corporate managers, however, the idea of social objectives that have real operational content is a novel and slippery concept. Social objectives have not been defined in most organizations' prior business practice. It is, of course, true that some corporations have long had "Ten Commandments"-type professions of business conduct in such areas as fair dealing with employees, customers, and suppliers and assurance of product quality and safety. However, recent revelations of business behavior that even friendly observers regard as marginal or reprehensible suggest that while moral creeds may have been sincerely articulated, they have not been administered with the systematic discipline that is applied to annual operating budgets. The record also suggests that operating managers often encounter difficult conflicts between the admirable standards of business conduct described in company philosophies and official ethical precepts, on one side, and the pressures created by short-term financial goals and the realities of competitive markets, on the other. Trapped in these conflict situations, some managers are pushed by their organizations' reward-penalty systems and their own career aspirations to sacrifice principles to expediency. Managers could hardly be expected to behave otherwise, nor would their own superiors usually want them to choose principle over performance when the stakes are high.

There is another, more serious difficulty. Corporate good-conduct codes express the beliefs of management about morally proper behavior. They reflect concepts and attitudes that are generated internally in the context of individuals' ethical beliefs. They are not usually formulated as reasoned responses to managers' readings of external attitudes and needs that find expression among special interest activists and groups. To most managers, these external forces appear to be hostile to, or at least inconsistent with, the economics of the market system. Further, they appear to lack consistency and universality, rising or declining in intensity in response to changing economic conditions, evolving social values and priorities, and even isolated catastrophic events (such as a major oil spill after a tanker grounding or offshore drilling accident). It is easy to understand and empathize with the skepticism of business leaders who observe activists pressing for substantial investments in the interest of environmental hygiene or product safety while other equally aggressive groups (sometimes, in fact, the same groups) oppose the price increases that reflect the costs of complying with these demands.

The requirement is therefore not for more and better codes of corporate ethics that are internally developed and reflect management values. Rather, it is for the development of policies and programs that (1) are responsive to values emerging in the society expressed as expectations and demands for general business and specific-company behavior, (2) are feasible for implementation by the company in terms of both economic costs and meaningful results, and (3) can be incorporated and implemented within the organization's administrative system (including operational goals, performance measurement, and rewards and penalties).

Doing this will call for sophisticated opinion research that focuses on early, formative-stage identification of public opinion (expectations, attitudes, needs) related to business performance and behavior, and translation of perceived opinion into its positive and negative implications for corporate policies and programs. While changes in social views may occur in many functional areas with their special publics—for example, in marketing, finance, and personnel—the chief public relations officer alone is responsible for corporate relations with all publics, is in the best position to perceive multipublic cross-relationships, and possesses the professional communications skills to articulate the influence of opinion on action. These circumstances argue for fixing the responsibility on the chief public relations officer for serving as corporate sensor, charged with perceiving and evaluating the full range of opinion trends among all relevant publics.

Fulfilling this responsibility will necessitate establishing and maintaining a sophisticated early warning system that taps both in-company and external sources of information. An essential ingredient in this system will be sensitive perception of the transition from the first expressions of concern by elements in the society to organized and powerful efforts to use the legislative process—or the administrative, judicial, or even proxy process—to accomplish objectives that are not seen as attainable through business voluntarism. A useful example of what is at stake here is the perception of and response to organized consumerism by business generally and by individual companies. Only the naive believe that Ralph Nader invented consumerism. Rising concern about protection of consumer interests was abroad in the land long before Nader became a media character. Few in the business community perceived the significance of the movement in its early stage, however, or evaluated the power, timing, and range of impact of its thrust. Indeed, it can be argued that it was precisely the insensitivity and unresponsiveness of business to what was troubling a growing number of consumers that created the opportunity that Nader so dramatically exploited.

If not adequately responded to, rising public concern about significant areas of corporate social performance will eventually convert into mandated business behavior. Examples abound in such areas as environmental pollution, product safety, and consumer finance. This makes a persuasive case for informed corporate initiatives that will reduce the likelihood of compulsion. The more business is perceived as resistant to the social will, the more it will be identified as the adversary of the public interest, the more the credibility of business leaders will crumble, and the less will be the influence they can bring to bear in the design of public policy. Against all these undesirable developments, at least within the scope of the individual corporation, an effective early warning system, including both perception and evaluation, can make substantive contributions. To service this primary need, the corporate public relations function must be broadened well beyond its traditional mission of interpreting the corporation to the public and must undertake the task of interpreting the public to the corporation.

Public Relations Participation in the Decision Process

In the socially responsive corporation the chief public relations officer must be invited in from the cold. He must become an active contributor to the decision-making process that precedes the formulation of corporate policies and programs. To be a meaningful contributor to that process, he must participate in it. To participate constructively in the formulation of policies and programs that relate in any significant way to a company's social performance and the accomplishment of its social objectives, he must participate in all policy and program decisions because he possesses the information and the professional judgment essential to identify those policies and programs that are materially relevant to a company's social posture and action. Finally, to be accepted as an equal participant, he must possess the organizational status, the professional competence, and the confidence and respect of his senior management associates that will earn their serious attention for his counsel.

These requirements describe a revolutionary change in the responsibilities of the public relations function as it is currently defined in most large companies. They describe an equally revolutionary change in the experience, knowledge, and skill qualifications of senior public relations officers. What is involved is no simple transition from a passive and responsive mode to an active and participative one. Inadequacies in performance will be clearly visible to the top-management group, and negative appraisals are likely to weaken confidence in the need for including the public relations function in the corporate policy-making process. This would be unfortunate because participation by a broadened public relations function in the executive policy process is essential to bring social considerations into a decision arena that has been dominated by the familiar complex of economic, marketing, technological, and financial considerations.

While some individuals presently responsible for directing the corporate public relations function are surely capable of effectively implementing the radically changed level and scope of the function described above, others are not equipped to handle such an assignment. In a number of companies it will be necessary to assign to the senior public relations positions executives with a broader view of and greater sensitivity to the social environment than traditional communications professionals possess. The result may well be that an existing senior communications specialist will become second in command of the newly defined public relations function and will continue to perform assignments comparable to traditional ones. This would not be a novel organizational accommodation to fundamental change in functional scope. Examples of a similar adjustment can be found in the redefinition of the marketing function in many companies from its traditional sales management orientation to a broader emphasis on product-market strategies.

Sophisticated communications skills will continue to be important elements in the enlarged public relations function, in transmitting information to selected publics and in helping to influence public opinion. But the communications technician whose capabilities are precisely defined by that title is not a manager who can participate effectively in the decision process at the level of corporate policy. In the near term, the enlarged policy-oriented public relations function in many major corporations will probably be headed by executives whose prior experience has been in other functional areas.

Such an individual will lack the technical knowledge and skills of the public relations professional. He will have to rely on inside staff and outside agency support for the design and execution of communications programs of all types. If he is the right person for the job, however, he will bring to his assignment such resources as broad and creative general intelligence, sensitivity to and understanding of the phenomena of change in social attitudes and expectations related to business performance and the processes through which attitudes and expectations are transformed into action, ability to perceive and articulate relationships between economic and social objectives and strategies, and capacity for enlisting the confidence and respect of senior-management associates. None of these attributes has anything to do with such other public relations skills as knowing how to organize and run a successful meeting with financial analysts or how to get mass audience exposure for a new product on national television news.

Examples of what the public relations director in the socially responsive corporation must be knowledgeable about and prepared to become involved with have been reported by business and general news media in recent years. Are his company's personnel policies effectively executed throughout the organization, so that the risks are minimal of adverse publicity, fines, retroactive compensation, or mandated future quotas? If not, what action programs, supported by what measurement and control systems and motivational procedures, should be instituted? Where in its multiple relationships with various publics is his company vulnerable to confrontations with or critical attacks by special interest groups that would interfere with ongoing or projected operations, or compel unnecessary or inefficient future investments and programs? Having identified such vulnerable points, what should be done, by way of actions, preparations, or communications, to diminish or remove the threat? What are the social performance implications of corporate policies and programs under consideration, and what, if anything, should be done about the implications? Under what circumstances—and when and how—should his company take up and publicize a position adversary to that announced or threatened by a government agency?

When should the company publicly ally itself with and support a proposed government policy or program, even in the face of opposition by its competitors? When should the company make price, employee relations, or other decisions that are certain to affect short-run costs and profits adversely but probably will enhance the company's social performance in the judgment of important publics and, as a result, possibly will contribute to long-term economic gains?

If the requirements projected in this discussion are confirmed by evolving experience, comparable changes will appear in the content of educational programs available to students planning careers in public relations at the corporate policy level. Schools of journalism, public relations, and business, pooling their resources and also tapping other faculty resources, will serve a demand for curricula that include building blocks of economics, sociology, social psychology, the processes of public opinion formation and influence, and political and governmental institutions and their operations, in addition to much of the traditional content of journalism, public relations, and business administration programs. If even a few schools launch imaginative initiatives in this field, careers in public relations should become more attractive for the kind of talented young men and women who, until now, have looked at the function with considerable skepticism if not contempt.

New Dimensions for Internal Communications

In the socially responsive corporation internal communications between top management and all levels of lower management, and also with professional, clerical, and production employees, must be transformed in scope and sophistication. The traditional public relations internal communications assignment has been to transmit to selected employee groups clear and persuasive descriptions of corporate policies and programs relevant to their "need to know." The new assignment for the public relations function is broader and more complex. Critical elements in the organization's internal culture must be radically revised. Closely related to this task are educational and training responsibilities connected with developing among managers who interact with community leaders, interest groups, media representatives, or public officials the skills necessary for effective articulation of the organization's economic and social interests.

Modification of the corporation's internal culture is necessary because it influences the attitudes and behavior of all managers. The elevation of social objectives to parity with economic objectives cannot be accomplished without major changes in the prevailing organizational culture. Bringing about such changes is a complex task because the prevailing culture is the product of institutional history, deeply rooted concepts and practices, and familiar motivational systems, all reinforced by the "self-image" syndrome that imposes a rigid pattern on selection for promotion. Unless this thorny issue is clearly understood and vigorously addressed, the chief executive officer who is committed to matching social with economic performance will encounter delay, misunderstanding, resistance, and even sabotage as he undertakes to express his revisionist corporate philosophy through the organization's plans, programs, and practices.

The resistance of the prevailing organizational culture to radical change in fundamental performance concepts and behavior is demonstrated in all kinds of business and public institutional settings. It is internal culture that inhibits top management's effort to transform an engineering-oriented business into a marketing-oriented business, as evidenced by the Bell System's twenty-year struggle to bring about this kind of change. Many smaller technology-based companies have experienced similar difficulties. Cultural lag has inhibited the desire of many corporate presidents to transform their companies from domestic to international enterprises, or to centralize key decision making in a business with a history of substantial local autonomy. In the not-for-profit area, internal cultural determinants have supported stubborn resistance to the substitution of cost-benefit criteria for what are viewed as the "purer" professional standards of science, medicine, education, or social service.

The roots of such institutional cultures are tough and deep. They are nourished by established policy, routine practice, habit, perceived self-interest, personnel selection criteria, and management performance measurement and control systems. They are strengthened by a shared belief that the institutional culture is consistent with the dominant cultural pattern of the external society. The perceived congruence of internal and external forces contributes to a powerful sense of the "rightness" of existing arrangements and a commitment to their continuance. This combination of performance and belief stiffens initial resistance to change.

The fact that the proposed reordering of corporate priorities calls for a balancing of economic and social objectives, not the more radical substitution of social for economic objectives, complicates rather than simplifies the problem. It might be easier to transform a for-profit into a not-for-profit organization than to secure broad understanding and acceptance through management ranks of the proposition that coordinating social and economic objectives in corporate plans and programs is not merely good business but is essential for the continuance of the enterprise system.

No simple pronouncement of the new policy orientation by a chief executive officer will cause such a change in his organization's culture. Even the formal introduction of social performance considerations into the organization's planning system and their representation in short-run operating goals are not likely to accomplish the desired results. Indeed, the initial effect of such actions probably will be to create perceptions of conflict between individual and group goals, on one side, and corporate goals, on the other. Such conflict situations can be expected to heighten any residual skepticism about the sincerity of top management's commitment to social objectives and the feasibility of specific policies and programs designed to attain them. Precisely these circumstances have impeded efforts by both business and educational organizations to carry out equal employment opportunity policies in recent years.

What is required is a communications program that is comprehensive and systematic in its ordering of objectives, rationale, examples, motivational devices, performance measurement, skill training, and continuing reinforcement of all elements. The new philosophy that balances social and economic goals must be stated and thoroughly explained to all managers, and its application in divisional and functional areas explicitly defined. Since the initial reaction of many middle-level executives is likely to be skeptical, with superficial conflicts between social and economic objectives cited as evidence to support their disbelief, top management must articulate the case for its new commitment in detailed and persuasive terms and must support precept with example. A corporate commitment to equal employment opportunity does not acquire credibility until managers see women, blacks, and other minorities promoted to responsible positions in numbers greater than "window dressing" requires; and also until managers believe that their own successful implementation of the equal opportunity policy carries significant weight in performance evaluations and in the distribution of rewards and penalties. Similarly, a corporate commitment to full protection of consumer interests must be translated into operational terms in product design, warranties, advertising, and supporting service before middle managers will understand and trust the commitment and incorporate it in their own areas of responsibility.

Encouraging managers to adopt a more open and responsive attitude toward external publics and particularly toward communications media can be an invitation to disaster unless managers are thoroughly indoctrinated in the situations they are likely to encounter and the specific strategies and skills required for effective performance in these novel assignments. Most managers presently are totally without experience or training in dealing with the press, community groups, and public opinion leaders. They need help in raising their sensitivity to and understanding of nonbusiness interests and attitudes. Role playing in simulated confrontation situations is useful. So too are programs that strengthen managers' belief that this new dimension of performance is significant in advancing their own careers. An effective way to nurture this belief is for senior management to demonstrate its own commitment by exposing itself to the same indoctrination and training experience and by publicizing its action.

Throughout this reordering of corporate priorities and development of related concepts, attitudes, and skills, the ultimate key to sustaining credibility will be the articulation and demonstration of top management's belief that rational fulfillment of selected corporate social performance objectives is the most effective strategy for accomplishing economic objectives. Managers must be persuaded that this is not a temporary aberration in the normal operating pattern of a profit-oriented society, but another phase in the evolution of a society which possesses the power to define the franchises it grants to corporations and other institutions. Successful adaptation to these conditions of existence has always been a characteristic of creatively healthy institutions. Making that kind of adaptation in this instance will require commitment based on understanding throughout management ranks.

The total communications program outlined above encompasses the content of four functional areas that are often independently structured in major corporation tables of organization: public relations, government relations, management development, and internal communications. The case for a coordinated plan for such a comprehensive communications program is in no sense a proposal for disturbing established organizational designs, which may have valid reasons for their continuance. Careful consideration should therefore be given to the desirability of pulling all four functional areas together under the jurisdiction of a senior corporate officer who has the requisite status and competence to implement the critically important responsibilities.

The Enlarged Public Relations Function

The transformation of the traditional public relations function described in this chapter is of such magnitude in innovation and breadth of responsibility, as well as in requirements for new knowledge and skill resources, that it can be adequately expressed only in a redefined public relations function. The principal components of this function include:

1. Continuing monitoring and evaluation of social attitudes and expectations related to all aspects of the performance and behavior of business institutions. The evaluation should encompass the timing and intensity of social attitudes and expectations, the analysis of complementarities and contradictions among social forces and interest groups, and the interplay between economic needs and social needs, which are sometimes mutually reinforcing and sometimes in conflict.

2. Continuing analysis of the significance of social attitudes and expectations for existing and potential corporate policies, programs, and specific actions that directly or indirectly influence both the reality and the perception of a company's social performance.

3. Development of recommendations for the maintenance or amendment of existing company policies and programs, and also for the design of new policies and programs related to social performance.

4. Participation in corporate strategic planning with special reference to the identification of social performance objectives, the interrelation of social and economic objectives, and the development of strategies and programs involved in accomplishing approved objectives.

5. Participation in the assessment of performance against targets and in the consequent amendment of plans and programs as an integral part of the continuing planning cycle.

6. Direction of the design and execution of communications aimed at all relevant publics within and outside the corporation. This is, of course, the primary task of the traditional public relations function. The significant

228

issue is that in the new concept of the function the content of communications is the result of an analysis and decision process in which the public relations officer has participated and to which he makes important contributions.

7. Preparation (through "consciousness raising," education, and skill training) of senior corporate officers and lower-level managers to play responsible roles in communicating with various publics and in interacting with interest groups, media representatives, government institutions, and public officials.

Unless this transformed concept of the traditional public relations function—including the change from a passive and responsive to an active and participative mode—is a central feature of corporate structure and operation, the approach to social performance is likely to be deficient in its design and incoherent in its articulation.

11

Relations with Government

ONLY a few years ago it would have been appropriate to focus the discussion of business relations with government on the importance of corporate managers taking an aggressive posture toward government organizations, officials, policies, and programs. This central theme would have included an analysis of sensitive areas along the business-government interface. It would have emphasized the need to develop an understanding of the policy-making process in governmental legislative and regulatory bodies, the key role of legislative and regulatory staff personnel, the timing and placement of strategic interventions, and the skills involved in building constructive relationships with senior and middle-level officials.

There is little need for such a discussion today. Broad-based business organizations, trade associations, and senior corporate managers have developed a rather sophisticated understanding of these matters. Business viewpoints are currently articulated with greater clarity and power than in earlier years. The complexities of the democratic political process in both the law-making and the administrative arenas are understood by most senior executives. Even more significant, throughout the business community there is a general recognition of the importance of active participation in the policy and regulatory process and the organization of persuasive communication of business positions on public issues and proposed actions.

The prevailing business attitude of the 1950s and 1960s that found simplified expression in the passive philosophy that the business of business is business and the business of government is government has been substantially, and fortunately, abandoned. However they may regret the change, most corporate executives now know that failure to make a powerful presentation of their views at the right time and to the right officials opens the way for other interest groups to establish a dominant influence with, all too often, unfortunate results for business interests and even for the society as a whole.

Negative and Positive Attitudes

There remains, however, one fundamental deficiency in the business approach to its relations with government. If not corrected, this will severely handicap the ability of business leaders to formulate and carry out successful strategies for social performance. This deficiency is the common business commitment to a negative position with respect to practically all proposals for reform in areas where there is widespread public discontent. Business representatives are eloquent, and have learned how to be effective, in criticizing legislative and regulatory proposals for changes in the rules of the game for the enterprise system. In almost every area where pressures for reform of business behavior have made their appearance in recent years—environmental pollution, consumer protection, product safety, work-place hygiene, energy conservation, and others—the visible strategy of corporate leaders in person and through their organizations has been to oppose change. This strategy has often been effective in slowing the pace of change and on occasion has been successful in defusing clearly dangerous and inefficient proposals for mandating change. On balance, however, it has been a costly strategy because it has confirmed for a large share of the American public its residual belief that the primary business interest is in the preservation of the status quo with only minimum concessions to critics of corporate behavior.

This is not a fair perception of the real position of imaginative business leaders who have a thorough grasp of the new forces moving in the American society. Nevertheless, it is the dominant public perception, documented in numerous opinion surveys. Critics of corporate social performance have used the popular perception to justify their adversary position. As a result, efforts by business leaders to draw public attention to the extraordinary economic and social costs associated with rapid application of extreme performance standards in the areas of pollution, safety, conservation, and other reform target areas have been portrayed as unreasoning blanket opposition disguised as trivial technical objections. The resulting "we-they" confrontations have damaged the credibility of business leaders. Even the skill displayed in recent years by some executives in expressing their opposition to uneconomic and ineffective designs for improving the quality of life in our society has been identified as still further evidence of fundamental hostility to change by social Neanderthals.

This type of confrontation in which all movement toward improvement of the social condition appears to be generated by nonbusiness interests while all opposition appears to stem from corporate leaders is ultimately damaging to both business and the enveloping society. Every business success in exposing the dangers of trying to move too far too fast—in mandating inflationary investments in nonproductive equipment and in overloading the adaptive capacity of complex technological and social systems—has achieved tactical victory at the expense of strategic defeat.

A sophisticated conservative member of Congress has criticized the behavior of business executives in his district for their unrestricted negativism along these very lines. He observes that when legislation aimed at ameliorating some specific widespread social dissatisfaction is before the Congress, he does not lack for discerning counsel from corporate leaders in his constituency who point out the defects in the proposed bill. They explain to him in detail why he should vote against it. He values their advice because it often helps him to see faults he might not discover through his own analysis. But when he observes to these same managers that the problem for which the pending bill is a poor solution is a genuine problem that needs a good solution and when he then solicits their constructive help in framing such a solution, their typical response is to recommend inaction. In his view, this counsel could come only from people who do not understand that in pressure group, single-interest democracy social ills inevitably will be addressed by bad solutions.

Opportunities for Business Initiatives

Some managers would view as revolutionary the idea that corporate leaders (1) should take the initiative in recognizing specific causes of broad public discontent with business behavior; (2) should apply their understanding of the technological and economic potentialities and the limits of feasible remedial action, through both their own voluntary actions within the business community and, when necessary, through government legislation and regulation; and (3) should then apply their newly developed skills in government relations to press for the acceptance of workable solutions. The strategy is worth examining, however, because its effective implementation would counter the popular perception that business is indifferent to social problems and is concerned only to protect its established practices. It would have the additional advantage of entering practical solutions in the forum of public analysis and debate at an early stage when public attitudes are still malleable. Above all, it would demonstrate to the central group of interested but as yet uncommitted citizens that the business community is not simply a defender of the status quo. This would have the desirable side effect of helping to legitimize business opposition to ill-considered proposals sponsored by special interest groups.

The confusing current debate about technological, economic, and social considerations associated with energy offers an interesting field for speculation about the possibilities for business initiatives. The energy debate has been dominated by narrowly focused environmental groups almost all of which have exhibited acute tunnel vision and lack of broad social concern with respect to the implications of their proposals for economic growth, productivity, jobs, living standards, and redress of the disadvantaged position of minorities. With few exceptions, each of these groups has tended to identify with a unique alleged benefit and has resisted efforts to extend the scope of its analysis to include either priorities among multiple benefits or trade-offs among related benefits and costs. Antinuclear groups concentrate on risks associated with atomic power plants and the disposal of radioactive wastes, without regard for the pros and cons of other sources of energy. Those concerned with health hazards associated with burning of fossil fuels resist invitations to consider the relative benefits and costs of alternatives. Solar enthusiasts focus on issues of safety and absence of pollution to the exclusion of the economics of the relevant technology and even of the realities of developmental lead times from pilot plant to full-scale application.

Business has responded to these aggressive claims, to be sure. With few exceptions, however, the responses have dealt with the issues in the same isolated fashion in which they have been argued by proponents. Thus allegations about the risks of nuclear power have been refuted with references to the safety of nuclear performance (at least until the Three Mile Island experience). Claims about the health hazards of fossil fuels have been countered with arguments about the limitations of state-of-art technology for removing the causes of health hazards and the costs of installing and operating this technology. Extravagant projections of solar applications have been questioned on feasibility grounds. On the largest stage set of all, a so-called federal energy program, itself no better than a disheveled patchwork of accommodation to selected environmental and business interests, for the most part has been debated on the business side item by item rather than in relation to the aggregate energy needs, costs, and risks of a complex industrial society. Business criticized the administration for not designing a genuinely comprehensive energy program. But it did not present its own program. The fragmented debate over objectives and methods was the inevitable outcome.

Another example is offered by the experience of the automobile industry with the tailpipe emission issue. The growing public concern with this special area of environmental pollution was apparent long before the enactment of legislation and the consequent aggressive rule making of the cognizant regulatory agency. The automobile industry's strategy, whatever its technical foundation, was perceived by the public as characterized by disinterest, delay, and outright opposition. In the general debate over standards, ways and means, and timing, the credibility of the industry's arguments was further weakened by the industry's successive steps of yielding and adapting under coercive pressure. What emerged from this course of behavior (which appeared to be a series of opportunistic concessions rather than a carefully designed strategy) was an unfortunate picture of an industry that was (1) insensitive to a matter of broad public concern, (2) unwilling to come forward with its own constructive program for ameliorating a disturbing condition, (3) hostile to governmental intervention, (4) deceptive in at least some of its claims of technical and cost barriers to compliance, and (5) generally an adversary of "the public interest."

That this is an unfair and misleading portrayal of the real attitude of senior automobile management is immaterial. It is the message that the industry's behavior over several years communicated to the public, as opinion surveys demonstrated. This perception wounded the credibility of automobile management with respect to the emission problem. The loss of credibility inevitably extended to other issues of great concern to the industry, such as fuel economy. Nor has the damage been confined to the automobile industry. It has weakened public trust and confidence in the business community as a whole.

An alternative scenario for handling the tailpipe emission problem can be sketched retrospectively. Starting with early identification of the emerging issue as one of potentially important public concern, the industry could have taken the initiative in claiming an interest at least equal to that of any external pressure group, reinforced by superior knowledge of technical feasibility and economic costs. The industry could have proposed its own emission reduction program and argued for its acceptance on specific engineering and economic grounds. However the program might have been modified in the ensuing debate, it would have enjoyed the advantage of being the set of proposals about which public debate on goals and means was conducted. Even more important, it would have given the industry the opportunity to lay out the facts about technology and costs comprehensively, which proponents of emission reduction from outside the industry lacked both capability and interest to do. Finally, an initiative of this character would have helped to build credibility and respect for industry leaders among influential elements in the general population who, unwillingly and unhappily, often have been pushed into criticism of the automobile industry's behavior precisely because they do not see the industry taking the initiatives they want and expect to see it take in the social performance area.

A third example may be of greater current interest because it is still in process of development and susceptible to strategic innovation. This is the response pattern of the cluster of industries involved in advertising to consumers as they attempt to deal with public pressures for controlling various aspects of advertising. While some advertising practices have been a target for criticism for decades, the pressures for change were not strongly organized or sharply focused. In general, the three industry groups concerned with the issue—advertisers, advertising agencies, and advertising media—were able to treat the criticism as largely emanating from social eccentrics who did not understand or were hostile to the competitive market system. Industry leaders generally paid little attention to specific complaints and made no significant effort to modify profitable practices.

The emergence of an organized and politically sophisticated consumer movement in recent years has radically changed this environment. One new element has been renewed interest in the methods and content of advertising. The growing dominance of television as an advertising medium undoubtedly has contributed to the intensity of the criticism because it has made exposure to commercial messages almost inescapable. There are now powerful pressures, some already generating legislative and regulatory remedies for alleged ills, for more "truth" and specific product performance information in the content of advertising, stringent curbs on television advertising directed to young children, and (the pressure here is less clearly articulated but emerging) limitations of one kind or another on the total quantity of advertising.

Industry's strategy in responding to these pressures is still evolving. There has been a substantive move toward a measure of self-regulation, accompanied by an effort to persuade the public that advertisers, agencies, and media are sensitive to their social responsibilities in handling such a powerful marketing instrument, and that voluntary self-regulation, properly designed and implemented, has a number of inherent advantages over government regulation. What is lacking in this response to date is anything in the nature of a comprehensive and specific program with identified goals and accountability for their accomplishment. As a result, a single business view of consumer advertising has not been clearly articulated, advertisers' credibility as proponents of self-reform remains at a low level, and pressures continue for governmental intervention.

The feasibility of a voluntary program to remove or ameliorate the most objectionable consumer advertising practices is debatable. There are substantial differences of opinion among major advertisers of consumer products about the seriousness of the threat posed by consumer organizations that are lobbying for legislative and regulatory remedies. There is also a degree of diversity of economic interests among advertisers, agencies, and media that impedes the formulation of a common social philosophy and a common program for its implementation. Nevertheless, there is an opportunity, which the evolving scenario of pressure and response has not yet foreclosed for business, to establish a constructive leadership posture. The goal would be to focus the discussion on a realistic set of remedies proposed by the industries whose social behavior is under critical attack, rather than on the extreme measures advanced by well-intentioned or even hostile reformers. Unlike some other areas of social discontent, consumer advertising is still open to business initiatives, although the time horizon for positive action is shrinking.

The handicap imposed by the diversity of interests involved in the consumer advertising issue might provide an opportunity for a business organization such as the U.S. Chamber of Commerce to assume a leadership role. The Chamber is in an advantageous position to accept and implement this responsibility because it has already undertaken to define a business strategy in relation to the full range of consumer interests. It has the additional resource of a professional staff with a sophisticated understanding of the influence of interest groups in our society and of the political process.

Designing and Implementing a Positive Strategy

A positive approach by business leaders to public dissatisfaction with business behavior is easier to recommend than it is to design and execute. In the past, most senior managers have tended to view with a degree of distaste approaching revulsion the legislative and regulatory bureaucracy. Some of this negative attitude persists, although it appears to be dissipating. In encouraging a positive attitude, what needs to be grasped is that there are two distinct but related levels of potential business contribution. One is the level of policy formulation, the other that of technical implementation.

On the policy formulation level, business is at least as well equipped as any other interest group, and as vitally concerned, to debate the scope and character of public policy as it might be applied to all aspects of corporate behavior and to attempt to focus the analysis on a reasonably balanced consideration of economic and social costs and benefits. On the technical implementation level, the potential business contribution draws on clearly superior resources of practical knowledge. As the legislative and regulatory processes work, unfortunately but apparently inevitably, nonparticipation or a visibly negative participation by business in the policy debate results in a rejection of later efforts to play a constructive role in the design of policy implementation techniques. It is therefore a losing strategy for business to argue, with respect to a serious problem of broad public concern, that the issue is trivial or that all remedial proposals are faulty, and then, when a policy decision has been made, to announce that only experienced managers are competent to advise on how it should be implemented. Such a strategy can only invite widespread distrust. This is precisely what has occurred in a number of areas in recent years.

Business participation in the formulation of public policy in every sensitive area of corporate social performance should be recognized as an advantageous strategy for three reasons. First, it is simply an exercise of good business citizenship to help to formulate policy decisions that may materially affect the quality of life, standards of living, material and product costs and prices, rules and procedures governing business operations, and the criteria by which corporate behavior will be evaluated and, in the last analysis, rewarded or penalized. In a society in which a major share of the human condition is influenced directly by the economic and social aspects of work experience in corporate organizations, and indirectly by the standard of living made possible by that work experience, it is neither reasonable nor prudent for the business sector to abstain from the public policy process.

Second, participation in the policy formulation phase of prospective governmental intervention affecting corporate social performance is likely to be the only valid admission ticket to participation in the policy implementation phase. Those who argue the case for nonintervention by government in any specific social performance situation lack credibility when they offer their services as technical counsel on questions of how best to accomplish an approved policy objective.

Third, business has a uniquely valuable ability to contribute to the design of systems and procedures for social engineering. It is relatively easy, for example, to reach a

241

public policy decision on the general question of taking some type of action to reduce environmental contamination. The complexities arise when the question is asked: What is the most effective way to reduce how much contamination when and in what circumstances? Such a question forces specific technical and economic issues to the surface. Do incentives or penalties or some combination of the two motivaters offer the best approach to stimulating desired action by contaminators? How do costs and benefits trade off along the path toward total decontamination? What are the limits of available technology in specific decontamination situations, and what are the prospects for advancing technology or reducing economic costs over what time span? Since many solutions to social ills, like many therapeutic drugs, have undesirable side effects, what controls or limitations should be imposed on specific decontamination programs?

One could readily develop a comparable list of operational questions for practically every corporate social performance issue, including those that are totally people-oriented such as nondiscriminatory personnel practices. And in every one of these issues there is a unique competence within the business community to contribute to the design of efficient and effective policy implementation procedures. It is advantageous for the society as a whole, not merely for the business sector, for this competence to be used. This is the heart of the case for a positive business strategy.

In evaluating ways and means of applying a positive business strategy in interacting with government, it is essential to push beyond the popular but superficial view that personal relationships with key legislators, agency officials, and their senior staff people are the critical channels through which influence over the public policy process is successfully exerted. That such relationships are both useful and necessary is beyond dispute. One cannot influence public policy decisions unless one can communicate with those who are directly involved in making the decisions. Frequently, however, communication process gets most of the attention while communication content gets all too little. This skewed emphasis explains the common complaint of members of Congress and their senior staff aides directed at corporate executives and their Washington representatives: "I know what they are going to tell me before they open their mouths, but they don't help me solve my fundamental problem, which is to solve the problem of some of my constituents."

Sophisticated observers of the governmental process know that the success of many special interest groups (including a number of those concerned with issues of corporate social performance) in attaining their legislative and regulatory goals is attributable less to carefully cultivated relationships with legislators, officials, and staffs than to three other factors. The first is that they focus on problems that are very important to clearly defined groups of citizens. The second is that they propose specific remedies to be implemented through legislation and regulation. And the third is that they organize concerted "grass-roots" campaigns in support of their programs. Their representation on the Washington scene, by and large, does not compare in scale, financing, and status with business (or, for that matter, labor) representation, and their personal relations with key officials are also less impressive. But they have cohesive constituencies that want specific relief or assistance, they recommend well-defined programs to achieve their objectives, and they organize powerful voter support in legislators' home districts.

There is an important lesson for corporate leaders in this record. It is essential that the business interest in our society reinforce the credibility of its concern about social issues, particularly those issues that are related to corporate behavior. To do this, the adversary or minimum-cooperation attitudes that have been widely perceived as characterizing much business behavior in recent years will have to be modified. These attitudes encourage distrust. They fuel the criticism of corporate performance by antibusiness activists. They also contribute to a general lack of public confidence in business intentions. Millions of citizens who, at best, are only vaguely knowledgeable about critical cost-benefit imbalances find it difficult to believe the public statements of corporate spokesmen. In this setting, statements by automobile executives about technical and economic constraints on the elimination of tailpipe pollution, by electric utility executives about trade-offs between additions to generating capacity and environmental contamination or safety, and by consumer industry executives about product purity or performance are simply not trusted. Too many in the audience recall earlier business hostility or indifference to public concerns about these issues.

In short, it is the worst possible long-range strategy for business to allow itself to be perceived as opposed to important interests of the society that holds ultimate power over the terms under which business functions. A healthy and prosperous business system cannot survive within a society in which large numbers of people perceive the private interest of business as opposed to the public interest of a majority of the citizens.

Since the public interest in a democracy seeks its satisfaction through governmental institutions and the political process, business must demonstrate its concern with the public interest in the same arena. The degree of confidence and trust business captures will be largely determined by its ability to propose constructive solutions for social problems that involve corporate behavior. Some executives may view this judgment as thoroughly unpleasant. Others may regard it as presenting very difficult tasks that few corporate leaders are presently prepared to handle competently. Both assessments are probably accurate. But there is little reason to conclude that there is a feasible alternative to the decision to organize to do the job thoroughly and well.

12

The Adaptive and Creative Corporation

T HE genius of American capitalism has been its ability to respond adaptively and creatively to changing conditions. This ability has been applied in responding to economic and technological developments arising outside the corporation and also to administrative challenges generated within the firm by expansion in the scale, scope, diversity, and complexity of operations. The same ability directed toward the management function itself has guided the evolution of management practice from its early intuitive tactics to its present state of professional art reinforced by a growing element of scientific discipline and technique.

The genius has been both adaptive and creative in significant combination. Perceptive executives have continually sought for ways to accommodate management practice to changing conditions external to and within their organizations. The most creative managers have looked beyond adaptation to change in their effort to discover ways to take command over change in order to administer it as a business resource. When steam technology became available in the early nineteenth century, it was advantageous for factory managers to adapt their operations to this new energy source. But it was genuinely creative, far beyond simple accommodation, for a few managers to invest in research and development aimed at rapidly increasing the capacity, efficiency, and flexibility of the new resource while concurrently redesigning production processes to facilitate full application of advancing steam technology and distribution systems to gain access to markets for the volume output of mechanized production. It has been advantageous during the past twenty-five years for managers to apply appropriate computer equipment in business information and control systems. A few extraordinarily creative executives have found it even more valuable to develop novel management structure designs and innovative decision procedures in order to exploit more fully the unique information-processing capabilities of computer technology.

In every business situation in which change occurs as a significant factor, there are, of course, a few managers who refuse to consider adaptive, much less creative, strategies. For example, when the right of employees to organize and bargain collectively about wages, benefits, and working conditions was first assured by federal legislation in 1935, some corporate leaders refused to accept the new relationship. Most of their peers began, however reluctantly, to focus their attention on ways of adapting their administration of labor relations to the requirements of the law. Initially a few and later a growing number of corporations developed a more creative view, exploring with responsible union leaders common problems to whose resolution both management and labor might contribute and shared interests from which both might benefit.

Similar divisions among opponents of change, reluctant adapters to change, and creative exploiters of change can be identified in business responses to every significant economic and technological development. The historical record is reasonably persuasive that organizations that have been adaptive and creative in responding to change have been more successful than the resisters. The record is also clear that the disposition and ability to design accommodative and creative responses to change have been key resources in the unparalleled long-term progress of American capitalism. In a literal sense they have constituted its unique genius.

Responding to Social Change

The changes in corporate social behavior for which there are now societal pressures obviously differ in content from the economic and technological changes with which managers are familiar. But there is nothing novel about the underlying problem: how to deal with an emerging new set of conditions for business operations. The challenge to business arising out of the current pressures has presented a comparable array of response options, ranging from total opposition on grounds of principle and expediency through degrees of accommodation all the way to creative initiatives that seek to exploit opportunities for constructive participation in and influence over social performance policies and standards.

The same ability to generate adaptive and creative responses to change that has been such a valuable management resource in the economic and technological arenas can be applied in the social arena. And there is the same powerful motivation for applying it—simply that the continued health and successful development of American capitalism depend on its satisfactory service of the needs of its host society. If that society, rightly or wrongly, becomes dissatisfied with the way business services its requirements, it will act to protect its perceived interests through alternative arrangements. In the worst-case situation, such action could be destructive of the business system itself.

There is neither need nor reason for enlightened business leadership to permit this worst-case situation to develop. The demands for social performance present as many opportunities as threats. Sophisticated managers can disentangle opportunities from threats and can design appropriate strategies to exploit opportunities and other strategies to ward off threats. Above all, they can establish an activist posture with respect to the formulation of social policy affecting corporate performance. They can inform public understanding of the relevant benefits and costs. And they can help to design effective and efficient procedures through which evolving public policy affecting business is implemented. In these constructive ways they will also contribute to strengthening public confidence in and respect for the role of business as a responsible participant in our evolving society.

The Critical Questions

The social changes that are roiling the current business environment require hard thinking about critical choices. Is the pressure for changed corporate social performance a temporary phenomenon? Or is it likely to persist and even expand into new areas that have not yet captured public attention? If it does persist, what are the options for corporate management? Are there realistic choices about social objectives and the means for attaining them? Can corporate management influence the process through which goals and implementation procedures are formulated? How can business leaders participate constructively in this process?

The central theme running through all these questions is the inevitability of the societal thrust toward a new social contract with business. If this thrust is appraised as a passing phenomenon stimulated by a small number of activists and their followers in an environment influenced by transitory economic and social conditions, vigorous opposition by corporate leaders to all or selected demands might be a rational general strategy. This determination is particularly significant in light of the fact that a large-scale corporate commitment to social performance programs undoubtedly will inflate costs and prices and probably will result in a lower rate of long-term growth in GNP.

If a contrary judgment is made about the pressures for changed corporate social performance, then a business strategy of opposing the desires, expectations, and demands of large segments of the public could cripple the private enterprise system. The historical record is clear on one point: what a majority of citizens in a democratic society want they will ultimately get, even if at a price they might not have been willing to pay had they been aware of it in advance. In such a situation, business really has no choice. Social forces and, as they ultimately become, political forces are as real and as potent determinants of business operations as are economic, technological, and market forces. Business must be responsive to them. The real task is to design and execute responses that effectively satisfy both social and business requirements.

It is on the basis of this proposition that it can be argued that commitments by business to properly designed socially responsive policies and programs will be profitable in the long run because they will help to maintain an overall environment in which business can continue to function with the degree of freedom and public confidence it needs. Even some increase in costs and prices and some curtailment in the rate of GNP growth may make sense if accompanied by generally desired improvements in the quality of life. (This judgment suggests that it may also be useful to develop an enlarged concept of GNP that includes measures of gains along a quality-of-life dimension.)

Those who share this view may conclude that the position of the outright critics of the concept of corporate social performance is fundamentally weak. Business may have no viable choice other than to accept social performance as a responsibility parallel to its traditional responsibility for economic performance. In this context, the critical issues for rational managers will be (1) identifying social expectations and demands related to business behavior, (2) determining feasible responses (whether by a single company, by cooperating groups of companies, or through governmental intervention, which business can help to shape), and (3) proceeding to implement preferred responses as efficiently and effectively as possible.

This view is reinforced by a number of recent and current economic, technological, social, and cultural developments that singly and in combination appear to be transforming our way of life so much and in such ways as to render a purely economic performance responsibility for business generally unacceptable to major elements in our society. These developments include:

1. Widespread recognition that the domestic supply of

natural resources to support industrial growth is finite, and the accompanying recognition that the United States is to a significant degree in transition from the status of a nation that enjoys substantial economic independence to the status of a nation that is significantly dependent on other countries for many essential resources. Closely tied to this development is the recognition that cost and other considerations related to all energy sources are likely in the years ahead to bring about important adjustments in industrial organization and structure, in living costs, and in the character of the national culture. All of these developments will disturb normal market relationships and invite (some believe compel) government intervention in some market activities to assure equitable distribution and protection of noneconomic interests.

2. Widespread recognition that unrestricted functioning of many extractive and manufacturing industries can exert damaging, dangerous, and in some circumstances lethal effects on the general environment and, directly or indirectly, on public health.

3. Widespread recognition that aggregate economic growth does not ultimately penetrate all parts of the nation, nor is it shared by all groups and individuals. We are now becoming vividly aware of the continued existence of deprivation for some in the midst of plenty for others, amounting to a poor nation immersed in a rich nation and struggling to escape from its restricted condition.

4. Increasing acceptance of the proposition that with power goes responsibility for its use—a proposition tied to the growing recognition that business, notably big business, possesses great power in both economic and social spheres.

5. Increasing acceptance of a cluster of beliefs about primary economic and related rights that should be guaranteed to all members of the American society, gen-

erally encompassing freedom from all types of discriminatory job and career experiences.

These developments give credibility to a projected scenario for American society in which the demand for changes in the social performance of business will continue strong, although with many possibilities for variations in the character and timing of specific goals and in the methods adopted for their accomplishment. There are, to be sure, important speculative issues. We cannot make confident judgments about how the public's discovery of the real economic and social costs of some social performance programs may affect the general will to insist on their implementation to the extent, in the manner, and at the rate originally projected. Some of these uncertainties have already surfaced in the environmental and energy areas. Others may appear in the product safety area. Even in the sensitive "personal rights" area we are encountering difficult issues of balancing equities among those seeking rapid removal of prior disadvantages and those whose opportunities may be curtailed by such redress.

Imperatives and Options

Both the general line of anticipated development and the possibility of modulations in its content and timing present opportunities and threats for business. In assessing the significance of these challenges and how to respond to them, corporate leaders will find it helpful to construct their analysis on the following three bedrock propositions:

First, adding social performance objectives to economic performance objectives does not mean and should not be allowed to mean abandoning or modifying long-run profit maximization as a primary management responsibility. An unprofitable or economically ailing business is not a social asset. Only a healthy business can generate the resources and provide the management skills required to mount and sustain significant social performance programs.

Second, it is totally unrewarding for the management of any company to consider social performance in general terms, lacking precise definition. Realistic economic planning lays out goals, policies, and action programs that are uniquely determined in light of the specific opportunities and threats in a company's external environment, the specific strengths and weaknesses in its available and acquirable resources, and the specific values of its principal managers. Comparable specific and unique considerations should be the foundation of realistic planning for social performance.

Third, whatever decisions are made about social performance goals and strategies should be incorporated within the organization's total management program. This requires specific operating objectives, measures of progress toward their accomplishment, use of these measures in evaluating the performance of responsible managers, and inclusion of these evaluations together with evaluations of accomplishment of economic and related objectives in the reward-penalty discipline.

On the basis of these fundamental propositions, corporate leaders can deal realistically with evolving social attitudes toward the behavior of business organizations. One additional consideration should influence management decisions on how to respond to social pressures. Given the present relatively low level of public confidence and trust in business institutions and their leaders, it is reasonable to anticipate that the imperatives acting on business managers will increase in the years ahead and the options will decrease. To the extent that business is not perceived as voluntarily responsive to widely felt social needs and wants, its compliance is likely to be compelled by social pressures acting through the political process to create legislative and regulatory mandates. Precisely this kind of transition from business options to government imperatives has been occurring in recent years. There appears to be no reason to anticipate a reversal in this trend so long as the business community is perceived to be opposed to the public interest, or insensitive to matters of deep public concern.

Growth of imperatives accompanied by reduction of options would be a thoroughly undesirable and unfortunate trend for both business and society. Mandating business behavior without opportunities for business initiatives and constructive participation cannot fail to result in inefficiencies in resource utilization, unduly high economic and social costs, intensified friction among social groups, and mounting hostility toward a business system that is viewed as an adversary to the public will. None of these results are inevitable. Most of them can be prevented or at least diminished by appropriate business action to exercise options before they are displaced by imperatives.

A positive attitude by corporate leaders who grasp the genuinely revolutionary character of the current period of social change and who understand the value to business and its host society of exercising private options before they become public imperatives will go far toward assisting society in accomplishing its goals effectively and efficiently. It will also help to preserve the creative dynamism of the system of American capitalism and the economic, social, and political freedoms that are inextricably associated with it.

Pondering these critical issues, the philosopher Alfred

North Whitehead concluded, "A great society is a society in which its men of business think greatly of their functions."

Removing the dated sexist reference, which itself suggests one aspect of changing social attitudes, the judgment defines both the challenge and the opportunity for enlightened corporate leadership.

Index

PROGRAM FOR STUDIES OF
THE MODERN CORPORATION
Graduate School of Business, Columbia University

PUBLICATIONS

———

FRANCIS JOSEPH AGUILAR
Scanning the Business Environment

MELVIN ANSHEN
Corporate Strategies for Social Performance

MELVIN ANSHEN, *editor*
Managing the Socially Responsible Corporation

HERMAN W. BEVIS
*Corporate Financial Reporting in a Competitive
Economy*

COURTNEY C. BROWN
Beyond the Bottom Line

COURTNEY C. BROWN
Putting the Corporate Board to Work

COURTNEY C. BROWN, *editor*
World Business: Promise and Problems

CHARLES DE HOGHTON, *editor*
The Company: Law, Structure, and Reform

RICHARD EELLS
The Corporation and the Arts

RICHARD EELLS, *editor*
International Business Philanthropy

RICHARD EELLS and CLARENCE WALTON, *editors*
Man in the City of the Future

JAMES C. EMERY
*Organizational Planning and Control Systems:
Theory and Technology*

ALBERT S. GLICKMAN, CLIFFORD P. HAHN, EDWIN A.
FLEISHMAN, and BRENT BAXTER
*Top Management Development and Succession: An
Exploratory Study*

NEIL H. JACOBY
Corporate Power and Social Responsibility

NEIL H. JACOBY
Multinational Oil: A Study in Industrial Dynamics

NEIL H. JACOBY, PETER NEHEMKIS, and RICHARD EELLS
*Bribery and Extortion in World Business: A Study of
Corporate Political Payments Abroad*

JAY W. LORSCH
Product Innovation and Organization

KENNETH G. PATRICK
*Perpetual Jeopardy—The Texas Gulf Sulphur Affair:
A Chronicle of Achievement and Misadventure*

KENNETH G. PATRICK and RICHARD EELLS
Education and the Business Dollar

IRVING PFEFFER, *editor*
The Financing of Small Business: A Current Assessment

STANLEY SALMEN
Duties of Administrators in Higher Education

GEORGE A. STEINER
Top Management Planning

GEORGE A. STEINER and WILLIAM G. RYAN
Industrial Project Management

GEORGE A. STEINER and WARREN M. CANNON, *editors*
Multinational Corporate Planning

GUS TYLER
*The Political Imperative: The Corporate Character of
Unions*

CLARENCE WALTON and RICHARD EELLS, *editors*
The Business System: Readings in Ideas and Concepts